Jim Emm

C000023561

MY LIFE iN PiECES, POEMS AND PARAGRAPHS

VERSES, MUSINGS AND ORIGINAL
OBSERVATIONS ON A COMPLEX,
WONDERFUL WORLD

Jim Emerton

MY LIFE iN PiECES, POEMS AND PARAGRAPHS

VERSES, MUSINGS AND ORIGINAL OBSERVATIONS ON A COMPLEX, WONDERFUL WORLD

MEREO
Cirencester

Mereo Books

1A The Wool Market Dyer Street Cirencester Gloucestershire GL7 2PR
An imprint of Memoirs Publishing www.mereobooks.com

My Life in Pieces, Poems and Paragraphs: 978-1-86151-629-9

First published in Great Britain in 2016
by Mereo Books, an imprint of Memoirs Publishing

The address for Memoirs Publishing Group Limited can be found at
www.memoirspublishing.com

The Memoirs Publishing Group Ltd Reg. No. 7834348

The Memoirs Publishing Group supports both The Forest Stewardship Council®
(FSC®) and the PEFC® leading international forest-certification organisations. Our
books carrying both the FSC label and the PEFC® and are printed on FSC®-certified
paper. FSC® is the only forest-certification scheme supported by the leading
environmental organisations including Greenpeace. Our paper procurement policy
can be found at www.memoirspublishing.com/environment

Typeset in 12/18pt Bembo
by Wiltshire Associates Publisher Services Ltd. Printed and bound in Great Britain
by Printondemand-Worldwide, Peterborough PE2 6XD

CONTENTS

I

Life, the universe and a few other things

THE SPIRIT OF FREEDOM

I felt a rush of free air today,
and basked in a sudden inner glow of reality.
The butterfly that flew and the flower that grew
in the garden of my head
when not a word was said.
I scanned the sky from my inner eye,
and saw the wonder of the world in its ever-changing faces.
A walk through time and space
to a place beyond the race where life was sweet.

I did not compete in the game of life
that was the cause of so much strife,
as I felt the pulse of inner being
of rich reward and so much feeling
that filled my well to overflowing,
in the single span of a solitary man.

WONDERFUL THINGS

There is a higher place that draws me as a magnet of truth.
Beyond the word, the thought, the god
It is the feeling that poets, lovers and mystics seek.
The essence of man, the source of it all is a pulsating brain,
a tiny spark in the cosmic whole.
Men seek dominion to conquer the earth,
and leave a deluded footprint in the sands of time.
It is my destiny to be a man, to sing my song, to play my tune,
as one day when the light goes dim,
the candle flame will have snuffed right out.
Yet in this life I have burned with beauty,
in the torch of wonderful things.

THE SOUL OF TORMENT

What have I become to feel so numb?

My feelings have turned to ice, when once my eyes were alight.

This is the cripple's cross born of human suffering that keeps me from the sea of nothingness.

In the flame of hope, I cling to the dream that all will be well

after this dark, lonely hell

that fills the shell

with a sense of pain so grim and bleak from the fathoms of the deep.

I LANDED ON A STAR

I landed on a star, and fired it with beauty. United with the cosmos at last, my final resting place was at the seat of mystical awe and wonder. What more can we crave than to be united with the essence, the genesis of our earthly creation?

Some seek fame and material gain, yet it is a spiritual leap to aim to seek the nucleus of all creation as a worldly salvation. From the heavenly soul of my inspiration, the pulsating light of truth may shine on all eternity, in a poetic leap of faith and belief.

THE AWAKENING

Life on earth is a spiritual journey, for some knowing souls who sense the earth, feel the pulse and breathe the fresh air of freedom. The big outdoors, with the orchestra of nature, makes you grow with each bird that calls and the gentle passing of ethereal butterflies.

In misty, mystical mornings as wild goose calls echo in the dank air, and senses are satiated by beauty, you may feel a river flowing from within. My personality is a well of being that fills my head with soft and gentle pleasure.

Come alive, take a step outside and feel the joy of a little boy who runs and skips along the long road to freedom.

LOST AND THEN FOUND

When I was young, on the edge of darkness, about to abandon hope

Weight of the world on my shoulders, I withdrew behind a secret mask.

Alone and in a dream, I felt relief from a primal scream

That yearned to echo in the world out there.

Then, after the cold days lost in a void, I found someone to breathe life into the nothing I had become.

As the darkness turned to light, no more the curtain of gloom, as my eyes shone with new light, and I knew I was born again with you.

MR FANTASY (1)

Dear Mr Fantasy, take me away

To the light of another day

Sing me a song, play me a tune

as I dance upon the moon.

You light the fire of the flame that burns within the magic cauldron

The walls have tumbled, boundaries gone, in pure free air I float along.

I am the passion, the heart of desire, to fan the flames of my hellfire.

Above the cloud I gently float, a pure free spirit on ethereal wings

We have encountered a beautiful thing, and it brought me joy and made me sing.

DAVID BOWIE

He was a musical metamorphosis. Fascinating egomorphs emerged from a brain that generated a fusion of psychosis and genius. His creative visions, nonconformist and rebellious in spirit, transformed the cultural consciousness of millions of people. Now the mainstream join in celebration of a force so great that his artistic singularity will live as long as man can see, hear and appreciate what a beautiful human being his personality was.

THE KICK INSIDE

A man on the edge of darkness and facing an early departure may feel the pulse of life from deep within. Not the time for depression and self-loathing, once the survival rush is felt.

In a life of convention, thought control and the veneer of civilisation, some men come alive and are born again. I came to being a spirit alive and free in wind-blown desert sands and the vibrant oceans, where brilliant fish were exotic life flowing free on warm, soothing currents.

In my short ephemeral life on Planet Earth, it has been a joy to feel the flow, hear the tune and bang the drum of personal experience.

YOU SET MY SOUL ON FIRE

I looked at you and knew that for the first time, I was alive. In an electric moment, my destiny lay in diamonds in your eyes.

No more sadness, only the gladness of two spirits as one, eternal lights from the room of empty darkness.

A man must walk alone, until he finds someone to call his own, as the footsteps in the snow point the way to happiness.

It's you and me against the world, as our little lives unfurl. The ripples on our ocean are calm, as we prepare for the next wave, a crescendo of sensations.

WHAT THE EARTH SAID TO ME

I went out into the world today; the freedom tasted of reality. The rustling leaves of gnarled old trees as the whistling wind brought life to my flushing cheeks.

It is so intoxicating to breathe the pulse of life that oozes from the heart of the earth.

I love to remain in my one domain, where the wild bird flies against a stormy sky and the red deer looms, a ghostly spectre under the moonlight.

It is the dreams of men that lure them into the womb of wilderness, where they shake off stress and luxuriate in divine peace and solitude. The simple things reach the soul of man, unfettered and free in every lifespan.

MAD WITH POWER

They come and go, men, women of today and tomorrow, and oh what sorrow they bring in the paranoia which is their thing.

With charm, con and chicanery they worship in the art of slavery, where people are mere projections of a distorted ego.

They are intoxicated by a grand delusion of themselves, bringing subservience and obedience to the faithful. Heads of State start as masters of their fate, until the sting of reality and truth is felt, when the illusion of lies is rumbled and they fall, silently, to earth.

Perhaps you recognise the monster within at the heart of political spin?

STAR

A cosmic king is born to sing his sweet song, that is the echo of truth and beauty.

He sets the stage alight with tongues of fire from the depths of his soul and desire.

From the turbulence within, a flame is ignited to capture the ears and minds of men.

The sound that he makes tingles spines and vibrates with lasting truth, and is pure and sweet. In the palm of his hand, the crowd are at one, and from afar fall under the spell of a star.

As the sun sinks slowly down, the genius now rests beyond the range of ordinary man.

A HIGHER PLACE

Let us go to another place, way beyond the men below

To be transported from the dark

in the bright blue sky above the lark.

The music of the spheres is vibrating my ears like a drug in the vein, a sweet refrain.

As lofty spirits we will glide

with you alone right by my side.

These enchanted moments we will share,

the joy and magic without a care,

for all the others lurking beneath in so much pain, strife and grief.

We have tapped into another realm, where reality is the child of dreams,

Another place of heightened senses that fill the being with wonder.

DANCE OF THE ROBOTS

What has man created that is not automated?

As long as they serve the master and do not bring disaster, there is a disarming beauty in their synchronicity.

The only thing I fear is that man will hold them dear, at the expense of our own sanity,

the life and soul of humanity.

Objects of man's creation, they will not lead to salvation, as the essence of their invention is power, money in obsession.

What feelings of power and control of the people who hold the key to the sway and dance of the robots in the palm of their hand?

For heaven's sake, take a lasting look at the swan on the lake.

THE GREY MAN

Unobserved, alone in a drab world of conformity, he shrinks from the teeming mass of humanity.

No outward sign of the true nature of the depths within, from a well rich with genius.

In another life, he is a shining light of true inspiration.

What a contrast he makes to convention he forsakes, for inside this noble and great mind a genius is found.

The grey man comes alive in higher places, beyond the norm of everyday faces.

With the special forces he fights, on the very edge of life, in another world, where mind and instinct are the story of blood, guts and glory.

THE LIGHT

There is a light shining on me; it is the eye of destiny.

I look from afar and follow my star, to show the way if I should stray.

A voice within is the music of my soul, and the instruments within make me whole.

The whispering wind tunes my ears, sparkles my eyes and calms the fears.

Soft falling rain to ease my pain, in each caress of tender cheeks

as the glistening sun alerts my eyes, to the things I could despise.

In my singular lifespan I feel like a simple man who drank the nectar of life

and took his chance in beautiful romance, and in the dark and lonely night

saw the light of truth.

PRIMAL SCREAM

I lost face in a dark and lonely place

as my world caved in on the prisoner within.

The sky was angry, flushed with red as I hid within my bed.

Each drop of rain was an emotional stream

that flooded my soul with dread and fear, of the voices I hear

as they bring pain to my ears.

Nowhere to hide from the anguish inside, which tears at my sanity and soul, now in fragments of the whole that used to be.

To bring a little sanity, I walked away from the woes of yesterday, bursting out in a primal scream that echoed deep within.

GIRL AND THE SHADOW

The little girl watched aglow at the shadow she was coming to know. The stranger skipped and danced, alerting her trance, and mirrored her every move.

In a voice soft and sweet, she gave Granddad a treat, as the shadow came alive in the imagination of her eyes.

She loved him so, and was charmed to know

that her invisible friend was well on the mend, and having fun with them too.

WALKING AWAY FROM YESTERDAY

The days in the sun were so much fun

in the days of yesterday when I was young.

I came alive, a vibrant spirit; it was my pledge to feel the edge of every cutting blade, that was felt so deep, to raise me up from an earthly sleep.

I saw the wonder of faraway places, exotic lands and happy faces.

To deal with all the sensual excitement, now evolved into pure enlightenment, as I reflect upon the written page, the life within a worldly sage who contemplates the path he takes as he walks away from yesterday.

THE LAST GOODBYE

I want you to know that in the final glow

Of a love that could never die, this is our last goodbye.

When mountains crumble to the sea, there could be you and I in all eternity.

We took our chance in a beautiful romance, an exotic dance of unbridled ecstasy.

As one spirit, we sailed the waves, our very souls saved from earthly cares that rest in troubled minds.

Born on the wind, we soared as larks on angel wings. It was the story of our lives, and now we must wave our last goodbye.

FROM ANOTHER PLACE

I came from another place, with the moon in the sky as the eagles fly, in a world that knows no bounds, of beautiful sounds, as minstrels sing aloft on angels' wings.

It has no beginning, there is no end, on my imagination I do defend.

Over mountain and seas I go as I please, the spirit wide and free, a living fantasy.

In the setting sun it is so much fun, to dance around in the wondrous crowd, of all that is noble and great

As I lean upon the garden gate, absorbed in the secret gardens of my mind.

CELEBRITY

Celebrity is my game, egomania my name

as I flaunt it in the spotlight, a shiny star so bright.

The world applauds me, reveres, worships and adores me

as I sing my song, receive my gong, and adorn the tabloid pages.

But where do I go to in the far reaches of my mind, a performing robot, so spiritually blind?

I am a human, a little man, aware of a single, earthly lifespan.

It is wise to know that in spite of the show, my life is one small flame in the fiery furnace of humanity.

SPORTING HERO

I am a star who jumps so far, right into the public eye.

My charisma is boundless, the spirit is endless, a hero of the world

I am so bold and adorned with gold from records and victories young and old.

They call me a visionary, immersed in history, of all the ages with my face on the pages, of goodness and greatness, a man of many faces.

When the final countdown is made, the people will all say that I was a sporting hero.

ODDBALL

I am an oddball loud and clear, and I feel a little queer.

In the world of the oblique, I am unique, with the single furrow I plough with courage and knowhow.

When the day is done I want the world to know that I am a single so and so.

Compelled to express my verbal finesse, I flirt with an image, until the feeling is finished, from the deepest seam of my beautiful dream.

Convention I know not how to follow, of rules and norms of all that is shallow.

At the end of my time it will be sublime, in the final fall of a brilliant oddball.

THE BEST I CAN BE

I have flown like an eagle, soared like a lark, bathed in the oceans and lived in the dark.

In the cold light of truth, I have done great things, in mountains and woods and refreshing springs.

The places I have seen, a beautiful dream, have been the story of my life.

I know my chance has been full of romance, of wonder and joy, a spiritual boy

Bound for the fast lane of life, on the edge of a knife that cut deep into the vein of my being.

In all the pain and the faults I can see, I know I am the best I can be.

WHAT AM I?

I am a grain of sand in the dusts of time, that swirls in a cosmic mist.

My inflated ego, a ripple in the sea of human consciousness, is as tiny as it is grandiose.

Human minds are blunt tools, sharpened only by belief, arrogance and delusion.

We may hold dear a perception of our tiny microcosm, a little self dwarfed by an endless and unknown entity, which we find both wonderful and awe-inspiring.

As the night pulls down the curtains on another day, it is enough to know that I am alive, a tiny link in the great chain of mystery and otherness.

MR FANTASY (2)

In my time of need and in the darkest hour, he springs into life, to my eternal delight.

Filling my life with gladness, no more the pain and sadness, his flame and spirit fire my imagination.

To those who dream, in answer to every scheme, he is the joker, the provoker of all things both wonderful and beautiful.

This purest phantom appears only to the believer, the dreamer of another paradise, of good and noble things divorced from worldly sins.

EXORCISING THE DEMONS

They lurk deep within, the soul and sting of sin

They eat the mind in the darkest dream, a reality within a fantasy

bearing the scars of trauma and despair, nursed by torture and painful care.

They are the imprint of malaise, of society in a craze

for money, fame and power, of ego every hour

that squeezes the juice from every man, destroying souls as fast as it can.

Have you confronted your demons in the darkest hour

to be freed from their mighty power

to stand in the light of day, unashamed to say

that your spirit is free at the hand of ecstasy to rest in all eternity?

THE EMPTY SHELL

As I look inside the barren husk of a fallen spirit and a well of empty dreams, I sense the nothing I have become.

A spiritual vacuum is the final remnant of a heart broken, in the embers of a love that perished and died.

Lonely and lost in time and space, a physical automaton that conceals an empty shell alienated from the warmth and compassion of man.

I cling to a little spark that lies deep within the secret vortex of the brain. It is my final hope.

ALONE AM I

I am an island that stands alone, washed and cooled by turbulent seas.

In the foaming waters charged by the whiff of iodine, I sense a reality that ebbs and flows with the moon and tide.

The rising sun, my solar friend, for my very life I do depend

its soothing rays upon my face to shine, to capture this lovely moment in time.

In the teeming mass who may belong to a huge wide world, humanity strong, I know my place as a solitary man

As the piper calls the tune, alone am I to sing my song.

I BELIEVE

When I came alive in a long and earthly life, I knew that I believe

Not in gods or almighty powers, but in the sun and moon and beautiful flowers.

I hold the rain that falls in the palm of my hand;

do not attempt to understand

Why the wind blows and the fire glows, and the ice crystals cling to my ruddy cheeks.

In icebound sunsets and misty morns, I feel the power, the awesome presence of the cosmic whole.

I know my place beneath the stars, the lark that soars under heaven and Mars.

This wondrous journey I have seen in richness and in fantasy feeds me to the core, as I once more believe in me.

ICE MAN

He is so cool, the man with the ice in his eyes. Like a wolf on the tundra, the air he breathes is of snowflakes and crystals that sparkle in the Arctic sun.

Detached, aloof, in touch with primal elements, he walks alone in tandem with the earth, the sun, the moon and the stars.

The soul is deep, beyond the scope of common man, made rich and whole by a life on the edge, and in the fire of experience.

Our iceman, an enigma, walks alone, and cannot be known

by men who live by form, in blind acceptance of the norm. What grace and beauty are to be found in this man, so profound?

THE SEA OF LIFE

Afloat in calm waters, in escape from the froth of turbulence of a troubled life, I embrace the surface where the sun beats down, the fishes fly and the ozone clings to my nostrils. No more the shadow, the darkest night, now the days of spiritual light.

In the world it seems a man must dream, of the beautiful blue sea, escape from reality,

of the ticking clock, the time bomb of life, at the pulse of earthly strife.

I am at one with the ocean flow, its wonder to bestow; my soul is blessed in a world of unrest. As the cock does crow in the fields that grow, these are my days in the sea of life.

SUPERNATURAL

Bound by the cloak of humanity, numbed by a sea of convention, let us take a trip into another experience, one step beyond. Blow your tiny mind, light up the senses and inhabit a heightened world, of sound, feeling, imagination and being.

Beyond, the plough, the clod, the symbol of God, is the rush of personal truth, an inner reality. In a lifetime spent in the cosmic world, in tune now with senses unfurled, I feel the rain, the sun the wind as it meets my delicate skin, that masks the man within.

Beyond the stars, the compass of man, the supernatural may find its home, a place that leaves humanity alone.

IMAGE

I write my words for all to see in a visual ecstasy. These are the pictures from my mind, ethereal, so sublime.

In bursting images from within, released above my delicate skin, I praise the shadow illuminate the dark, the hovering kestrel, the lovely lark.

In higher feelings I sing my song, the world responds and makes me strong.

Yet can you see the real me or is the image a fantasy?

A man on paper and in print, who is the mystery that makes you squint?

From a voice within I know myself, a superstar, a little elf.

ELEMENTS I KNOW

It has been fun in the rising sun, the hail that stings on rosy cheeks;

It was I who knew the stream that flowed to cool my feet, out in the rain, the snow, the sleet.

In the outer world my spirit stirred as I came alive under giant Neptune, Mercury and Mars.

A day on earth, moments well spent to feed my soul with no repent.

A shooting star I see, a vision of ecstasy, as my love I found, in every sound, of the orchestra of nature, the holy shroud.

The wind did blow and the fire glowed within my eyes as the brain it flowed, with notes a symphony, of elemental harmony.

I am so blessed to have been possessed, and touched by a world of wonders.

THE MONSTER

Behind the mask of the common man, the conformist, a shadow lurks within.

In the dark pools of the psyche evil finds sanctuary, in the depths of the disturbed.

Relegated, repressed and supressed from obvious view, a ruthless intent may unleash the monster from within.

If it emerges into the light of day, maybe its destiny is to cause affray

inflicting pain and suffering on its stay in the masses of the day.

DREAM TO FLY

In the depths of the night or the light of the day I feel I can fly away, nothing to inhibit from the depths of my spirit, as she launches freefalling and somersaulting across the open sky.

The yogi, the seer, free from fear, may escape the body, the physical shell, the ego trap, the living hell.

To feel the colours, the warmth of sound, and be transported, a world of the profound

in pure euphoria I do fly, a purist spirit across the sky.

OPIUM

Be transported on ethereal wings, and float gently in a calming sea of euphoria. Dwell in a mystic feeling beyond words, in pure detachment from the world of man and things, in a beautiful dream.

It is a spiritual world that smacks of reality and eternity, induced by the wicked poppy flower. Be seduced by the soft blanket of self-absorption as you inhabit the magical world of trance.

MY BEAUTIFUL EGO

The essence of mind transports me to delights, and dwells in a world of unbridled fantasy. Becoming a reality of its own, and restrained by the brain, it shines bight like a diamond, and glows like a firefly, a transcendent creature in the sky.

The flowers that grow in sweet gardens of my imagination are the petals of poetry, the scent of a lotus. I float along on the whispering wind, a moment in time of the lark that sings, high in the bright blue sky.

My spirit knows no material things, it sings and dances with angel wings; as light as a feather, I am the pulse of butterfly wings.

SPIRIT FREE

It is a man's dream to escape the absurd, soar like a lark and fly like a bird.

Feel it, sense it, nurture it when you float like an angel on open wings

light as gossamer the heart it sings.

You have no boundaries, the rules have gone, this is your time, a sweet love song.

The eye of an eagle knows no fear as it pierces the sky, the running deer.

If I come down from this beautiful high, I shall not fear that I may die.

RECITAL LOST IN TIME

I stepped on to the stage in another age to bare my soul to the public eye.

Sweet delusion of a performing superstar, in a glorious rush of ego gratification.

In bitter sweet, self-critique, my best was in third place. Aeons later,

I luxuriate in the belief that my feelings as word projections are purer, clearer and peculiar to me. A lyrical journey of the self in pursuit of crystal clarity, the whole self for the world to see.

Originality is the pursuit of the lonely in pure defiance of convention, in a beautiful state of devilish freedom.

VOICES FROM WITHIN

When climbing paths to heaven's door

I saw Gabriel, and what's more

spiritual beings in an astral mist

danced for joy, embraced and kissed.

An inner feeling suffused my soul

Before I was part of an unknown whole.

An ant on a mountain without a hope

the subject of a microscope.

But now I'm vibrant, exploding with power,

transcending dimensions hour by hour.

I can see beyond the human mind

and find the secrets of mankind

All knowledge of universe has been unfurled

for I've been inside the spiritual world.

ECLIPSE OF THE HEART

In the pulse of my being is an icy emotion, the presence of a cold-hearted orb. It shines by night, to take colours from our sight.

Frozen, frigid like stone, and void of feeling, consuming the warm and friendly rays of summer sun, it masks and occludes my sentiments and feelings in an eclipse of the heart. Strange things in the mysterious microcosm of the human soul and the beating heart.

THE CANDLE OF LIFE

My little clock is ticking, an echo from the sands of time, like a fleeting moment of feelings so sublime.

I now reflect on ages past, crystals of beauty have filled my eye and I have kissed the sky.

The joy I have known, voices that resonate from deep within. Places I have seen, to fulfil my dream, of life betwixt darkness and light.

I saw the sun rise, the moon shine, and bathed in the warm embrace of summer rain. A tortuous fusion of genius and madness has filled my empty vessel with the fullness of truth.

PADMASANA

Flowing once more in the eye of another dream, I feel transported to another more lovely place. Far away from material constraints, I bask in feelings of cotton-wool clouds, of summer birdsong, and the gentle raindrop that falls from shimmering peacock eye.

My destiny is transcendence, the pulse of inner being liberated in a beautiful profusion of thoughts and images, as they erupt from the conscious whirlpool of the psyche. At one with myself, it brings me joy to know that I face sweet images, as a singular man, and that this feeling is mine alone.

NUCLEUS OF MY LIFE

A little child, born naïve and free and baptised in complexity, survived a sea of stress, a single life the test. Life became a labyrinth, as the great web of the world drew me into the inner core of confusion, as one tiny being struggled to survive the onerous and compelling influence of humanity.

The ubiquitous and mind-numbing thought control, the monster of education, stimulated a simple mind, unaware of the price paid to convention, simple awareness of freedom.

Now as the sun begins to set, my inner eye shines bright with a spiritual light, the soul and nucleus of my life, as I open my single page, it is the way of the sage.

THE CHILD WITHIN

Aloof, withdrawn, a chick inside my inner shell, I gazed upon the world with half-closed eyes. Little did I see of life's great mystery.

Then, as time flew by, I looked and saw a bright blue sky, the summer clouds and birds that fly, over forests so dark and deep, the estuary and tidal creek.

In a worldly flow, I came to know, at the gate of mystery, the teaming mass of humanity. My eyes once dim, to earthly sin, shone with crystal clarity, the reality sealed by the truth revealed.

And now with coming age, and clarity of the sage, I sense the child in my eyes once more, to give me joy, faith and light, and to point the way, a rebirth in the womb of nature.

WALKING IN THE AIR

Alone in my chair, I'm walking in the air.

As I soar up to the heavens, rise on a thermal and fall like a raindrop, I kiss the sky, for I am alive.

It was not always so in the dark days of yesterday, when things were nebulous, unclear

But now I'm vibrant, exploding with power, seeking new dimensions by the hour.

I sense the delicate rays of the winter sun, boys and girls having so much fun.

The days of my life are in full bloom, the fires glow bright, ignite the gloom.

My worldly story does unfold, I do not care about getting old

as I stop and stare

and walk right in the air.

THE ANONYMOUS CROWD

A seething mass of humanity, vibrating, jostling for position in the sea of life, makes me demented, anathema to my senses. They suck the life out of me, my sensitive little psyche. Air and space I enjoy, room to arch my wings, amongst each and everything. I feel so low that the spiritual glow, feels dim, as I retreat into the empty vacuum of vulnerable exposure. Give me the sanctity of my room, to shed the gloom and feed the inner man, to feel the warmth of my creative span. I love to shake off the death shroud of the anonymous crowd. This exposed, raw nerve is for the gifted who will feel it.

TRAUMATIC TEARS

Tears like mercury flowing from the concealed darkness of my melancholy are droplets of rain from the cloud of inner man. Gentle and pure, yet charged with emotion, they have the salty tang of reality. Each one has been created from the well of being, flushed by many thoughts, saturated in feeling. In pure catharsis, they run and are shed from my flushing cheeks. As time consumes my fears, kissed by traumatic tears.

THE OLD ROGUE

Lustful, lascivious and dissolute, lurking as a predator on the weak and vulnerable, he casts a sexual shadow over the fair sex. Cunning charm is at the core of this narcissus, spinning a complex web of lies and deceit inspired by Casanova. Fanciful and shallow, a reservoir of endless fantasy and broken promises and empty dreams, he chalks up another numerical conquest to satiate a hungry ego, ignited by the flames of mania. Flattered by his manipulative spell ,they fall for his self-conscious charisma.

MANIC DEPRESSION BLUES

Way down in my shoes, alone in my shell, I am under the spell,

the hopeless delusion that all is well. I try in vain to ease the pain, my little excuse for yet more self-abuse.

In the complex of my mind is a dark empty tunnel, my only relief from the vacuum of an empty being. My light is dimmed, occluded by an empty cloud, descending on me as a death shroud.

Is this my fate, a life's journey, the final sentence, a prisoner of the manic depressive blues?

A poem dedicated to all troubled souls who are gripped by torture.

THE MONEY GOD

Before you face the sod, bow to the money god

a life of material exploitation, devoid of sophistication

will earn you the right of death, the final reward of empty and lifeless things.

Before the final sting, you may see the glimmer of the light of truth, a nebulous sense of spiritual awakening.

A lifetime chasing the capitalist dream results in a genesis, an emergence of the butterfly of truth, which cloaks the seeker in pure magic.

Some, yet to realise the essence of life, will perish as slaves to the lord of illusion, the money god.

EVIL ON THE MOOR

We walk in the shadows of dark ages past. It is said that the ghosts and restless spirits of the past inhabit the moors, to claim the souls of the meek and vulnerable, lured on misty nights that envelope the moon in an evil aura of doom. If you but dare to test your fate and walk alone, rigid with fear, you may encounter the presence of evil, the awesome and satanic HAIRY HAND OF BODMIN!

Personal testimony of a brief encounter with the phantom may be given by Steve Wright.

THE INNER MAN

You may hunt high and low for the man who lurks below

In all sobriety forget society, as the voice of truth is deep within. My intuition is the light that guides my way in the lonely night.

When others don their masks to read, my spirit is set loose and freed, to wander into places new, known only by the chosen few, who dare to escape from the conventional norm, creative wonders to perform. A lifetime's searching lights my way, as the inner man is here to stay.

HALLUCINATIONS

What wonders to perceive in the flow of dreams. Raise questions of reality, our life and its finality. Fusions of sound and colour, they feel like no other in the kaleidoscope of the psyche. You feel you can fly in your mind's eye. Lie back and just float as the drug rocks your boat into the foamy waters of the rich blue sea. It will be so hip to emerge from this trip, no longer in fright but blessed by insight. Careful the doors that you open as madness is the token, the toll that you pay for a nice little stay into the world of surrealism.

MY PSYCHOTIC FRIEND

Emerging from the abyss, from the depths of the cauldron of fire, he ignites reality, breath of the dragon in conscious flame.

Distorting the senses with an intuitive perception, he shocks the mind into the light of being, and another psychic morph is born. His home is a brain charged by alchemy and electrical storms that flash like lightning in the mind.

My little friend gives weight and meaning to sanity itself, in waves of truth, and touches the essence of a human soul stripped bare to the marrow.

This is my dedication to all those who encounter their little mad friend.

MY CHEMICAL ROMANCE

Doors of perception, heaven and hell

are in the scope of my little spell.

The inner realm of a fluid mind

probing secrets of mankind.

The charade, the mask dissolve in a sea of clear perception

beyond the acts of human deception.

Beyond the plough, the spade the clod

an eagle soars in the face of god.

All is sharp and understood

I love this simple wonderdrug.

It yields transcendence, power and glory,

the object of my beautiful story.

It did not happen just by chance

My wondrous dream, my chemical romance.

MYSTICAL MIND

Beyond the word, the thought, the god, there is a realm that may be felt.

It dwells within the soul and depths, its own reality to cast its spell.

Complete and full the inner psyche

like the presence of the Lord Almighty.

Beyond the norm, the seat of convention, suffused by psychotic injection

It empowers and transports and enriches the being

as you float high up to the ceiling.

You cannot always reach this state

the very nature of your fate.

THE PIPE OF DREAMS

Breathe deep on the pipe of dreams, feel the spirit emerge from the egg of schemes.

Draw on the cool smoke of freedom, liberation from the conscious ego.

Transcendence is the word from a world of the absurd.

It is a trip into the sweet and beautiful flow of pure euphoria, which transports, delights and cleanses the soul of care and anguish

a mind now escaped from the prison of the ego.

A SHADOW OF WHAT YOU COULD BE

Timid little people, losing their spirit of freedom in the mass conformity of the day, keeping censorship at bay.

Subordinating themselves to conventions, collective beliefs, prisoners of their own grief.

The imagination is void of gleam, they have sold out to the mainstream.

Like the lesson of the moth, why not enter the light, and ignite the flame?

The empassioned craving of desire to be immolated by the flames of life

fuelled by the furnace of the unconscious mind.

Seek it, hunt it, the inner pulse of your being, and embrace life. Then you will no longer walk in the shadow of what you could be.

MR BARKING

It is no pretension that I inhabit another dimension

It is so sad that I am barking mad.

My tiny mind races to weird and wonderful places, in fantasy dreams and the irrational, because it's so very fashionable to be eccentric, wacky and quirky, and totally absorbed by cold turkey.

I drop a little pill again, to fuel up like Spike Milligan.

In pursuit of fame I go quite insane

as the men in white coats really get up my goat.

It goes without mention, that they favour my section

as they come to take me away

for a very long stay

in the home of lunatics, moonbats and monsters.

I know where I will be parking, cos I am Mr Barking.

THE OLD MAN

Body crumbling into decay, after a long, long stay nursed by Mother Earth

A life of unconvention yearning for a new dimension, and blessed by rich adventures, I have travelled far and wide, a lofty spirit in the sky.

I trod my path with a singular mind, so that life's secrets I would find.

The final solution is simple, a long journey to the temple, the integrity of the self.

In the looking glass I saw a face, an old boy of the human race

I realised in a while

and with a little guile

that it was me.

THE EDGE

Close to the wind, alive and exhilarated, taking a plunge into the unknown, alive on the edge of darkness, I step out into the night shadows of ancient Damascus. A pulse of wild tension, alive with expectation, courses my veins. Charged by adrenaline risk, I draw on the pipe of sweet enlightenment. In the roof of the world the old self, sealed by convention, is shed in metamorphosis, as the imago, fresh and pure, takes flight into the light of day, basking in warm sunny air. It is a spiritual rebirth, man reborn from a brief encounter with the edge.

ALIEN LIFEFORMS

The cosmos of which we are a part is beyond our human concepts of space, time and infinity. The collective impact of human consciousness, of science, cosmology and human effects is but a blunt tool in the perceived reality of cosmic existence. I do believe that with the shallow impact of man, we delude ourselves with the idea and arrogance in believing we have total knowledge of what is out there.

The quintessence of the cosmos is beyond sight and reason. However in historical time we have a nice collection of theories promulgated by academics, scientists, philosophers and believers in humanity. As a man my little belief is that beyond my perceived self, the cosmos just is. There is a possibility that alien lifeforms exist beyond our current experience and detection, perhaps in various forms which may be like those on earth or supernatural. Other dimensions of experience may exist in other universes.

It is certain that people think about these concepts as the microcosm aims to contemplate and understand the macrocosm. This seems valid, although it may be just a stream of consciousness in pulses from the brain/mind synthesis.

BEFORE THE BIG BANG?

Cosmologists attempt with their minds to know and determine the nature of the cosmos. The irony is that they are part of it themselves in a physical and non-physical sense, as the cosmos can be conceived as a unified whole. Sophisticated as science may be thought to be in the popular consciousness of the day, I would question the validity of the truth of the Big Bang as the origin of the universe, and the accuracy of timing of apparent historical events millions of years in the past. I ask the question as to the nature of the cosmos and existence before the BB, and without omniscience, how we can know the answers in relation to our human concepts of space, time, infinity, existence and non-existence.

To me it is counter-intuitive to think that we are separate from the cosmos we are trying to study and define. My personal belief is that the collective quest of humanity will not arrive at the truth in an absolute sense, since we are not omniscient and omnipotent. We know that science is but one human tool to aid some understanding of external reality and the human condition, others being philosophy and religion. I rest in my ignorance of anything in an absolute way.

THE OBSCURE NATURE OF FAME

A person in Ethiopia was reading my work, and this was significant to me. In all the places in the world where the writer's work is digested, the author remains unknown in all his complexity. We recognise and perceive an image, which may assume an identity of its own in the popular consciousness of the times. I am intrigued by the mystery of the individual within the cult of the celebrity. Every man is an island, and I feel it is important to maintain a sense of integrity and individuality in society.

People are often made famous by the media, which recognise perceived talent and originality. I believe many like a space of free air in which they function as a separate, autonomous entity, with insights this may engender. Many go through life without knowing themselves, yet alone others. However, the fame impulse can be the beating heart of the human condition, and most of us are conditioned by its influences, since humanity tends to be a social organism.

RISE OF THE MACHINE

When machines were mice and men were lions, we did not think of the times when technology would rule the minds of men as inanimate gods. Men need to tune into calls from the soul and the echoes of instincts deep within. In the deep-seated schism that divides men from their true nature, the computer becomes a revered object of love and devotion, alongside the shallow face of texting and endless utterings of shallow consequence. Oh for a love of all that is wild and free with a little spirituality, then we may see a little sensitivity, love and harmony in response to the rise of the machine.

COSMOS

How can I know the Cosmos, a greater entity than I? It is wonder that makes me gaze up into the sky. I light the flame from within my eye, to embrace an impossible journey, that leads back to myself. Much as we try to know of such things, the mystery remains, and the truth is shrouded by clouds of uncertainty. My little conscious stream is all I know, a tiny niche in a nebulous sea of otherness. The foolishness and arrogance of humanity will never know the essence of the great beyond.

THE QUEST FOR ALIEN LIFE

The curiosity of man compels him to probe the cosmos in search of non-human lifeforms or evidence of alternative sentience or intelligence. It may be possible, yet consider the possibility that there are none, even in the vastness of the space-time continuum. Often propelled by imagination and belief, man continues his search to test and find the limitations of consciousness, cosmology, science, technology and religion, all evolving under the cloak of humanity.

It is contemplated that cosmic life entities may exist in a form or dimension that are undetectable by modern, primitive man. A school of belief asserts that we are all descended from aliens. Perhaps we should align the search with the notion of a supernatural being or god. This is my little exploration into the little microcosm of my own consciousness, or is it?

PSYCHOPATH

The sweet-voiced charmer shields a ruthless soul behind the warm and radiant mask. It is the smile of evil intent from the firmament that lurks within. He will take you, break you and forsake you, as money is his game to fill the void within. The spiv, the sharpster, lurks in the shadows of his soul, you not to make him whole, as feelings leave him cold, the psychopath so bold.

THE HOUSEBOAT

In the wild, remote sea washes she was moored, facing the salt-laden winds, fresh with a tinge of iodine from the North Sea. It was a young man's dream to slip under the army blankets on the bunk and plan the next wildfowling foray into the saltings and the stalk edges. Silent contemplation and a soaring imagination were punctuated by the singular and rugged presence of the Wild Goose Man of the Wash. What wild adventures we pursued in icebound sunsets, in swirling winds bearing snowflakes that clung to beards and melted with the rush of warm air from nostrils. The Tilly lamp flickered as hardcase eccentrics exchanged colourful stories, fuelled by beans, soup and eggs rendered edible on a smoky paraffin stove. As the moon cast her melancholy light over the seascape, plaintive cries of curlew haunted the dank air, grey seals surfaced and little terns, so graceful and magical, dived into the icy waters below. The elements exhilarated as the spirit soared, leaving traces of wonder in an old man's reflections.

INSTINCT AND ACUMEN

I came alive on the edge of survival in the wilderness and faced with great difficulties in Afghanistan and an area of tribal law in Pakistan as part of my worldly adventures. It was thrilling and frightening to the core, and the stimuli yielded great insight that serves you well. The instinctual side of the self, similar to intuition, gives an instant perception of what you should take notice of. If clear thinking follows, then you may survive the threat or the dangerous situation you face.

With pigeons, try and align your instincts with each individual bird and the colony, to gain a perception and an instinctive understanding of the bird's potential, personality and some degree of predictability in anticipated performance at race points, particularly over distance and marathon events. The thinking man can ponder a method, a plan, yet sharp perception is instant.

ZEN AND THE ART OF LONG-DISTANCE PIGEON RACING

I am very fond of practising mindfulness associated with the fundamentals of Zen Buddhism. The essence is silent concentration and contemplation from within, ideal for the endurance/duration of pigeon racing over many days, and is how my writing and poetry are generated. A little counter materialistic culture, I promote this practice as often as possible in our earthly lives. If it suits, try some absorbed self-reflection to enhance focus and objectivity.

I started my habit at an early age in response to the wonder and beauty of nature and birds like Charlie Fantail at 4 years of age, some 62 years ago. If inclined to introspection and peace seeking I recommend this turning on technique towards inner spirituality. At the long marathon races over 700 miles you will need to refresh the inner core.

PRESCRIBED DRUGS AND IQ

When I took the Mensa test and scored in the top percentile, I perceived that on prescribed Amitryptiline for depression my brain/mind was superstimulated, enhancing concentration and self-awareness. Along with this I had switched down emotions and gone into a zen-like phase of focused mindfulness to achieve the objective. Perhaps this perception will stimulate a response from the reader, as I am now a writer/poet in many media.

MY LITTLE SUBCONSCIOUS PSYCHE

My creative quirks, dreams and purer feelings flow from subterranean depths, the inner well of being. I let them inhabit and flow into the conscious ego, the rational intellect that shapes it into poetic or comical forms, ideas and serious thoughts. The secret is unity, or individuation of the total being and comfortable acceptance in self-knowledge. It helps to be introspective and self-conscious to feel at piece with my travel into the microcosm.

PARANORMAL EXPERIENCE AND BELIEF

The world is a vast reservoir of stimuli, sights, sounds and experiences. In my extensive travels into it, and perception of my own psychic processes, I have encountered mind reading by a very perceptive man in Delhi, two out-of-body experiences which changed my deepest perceptions of life on earth as a person, and a shared consciousness with others. In moments of euphoria, mystical and elevated conscious states are not unusual. The above events are common to many people and perhaps other life forms, say elephants or dogs? I believe some powerful and supersensory, intuitive, perceptive and stimulated people can make what appears to be the paranormal quite usual – I suspect that some folk regarded as mad know many things.

THE MICROCOSM WITHIN THE MACROCOSM

A light, glowing bright inside my head, is my little perception of a vast, unknown cosmos. I cling to my inner vision, as it is the only reality and truth I know. In the vast sea of humanity, we jostle and swirl around in a vortex of ignorance. Deluding ourselves with ego, culture and belief, we can but aspire to knowledge of ourselves, a minuscule microcosm on an earthly speck in the vastness of the space-time continuum. In brief moments of insight we may stand at the gate of mysticism in the beautiful and absorbing fact that we know nothing, that the illusion of the ego has told us to be true.

THE SUPERNATURAL AND PIGEONS

As a young man the birds fired my enthusiasm to a very high level, placing them above all. They were at the core of all my aims and ambitions. With an intense feeling, I sat up in bed with a vision, a stream of consciousness depicting a montage of the future with my dark chequered family. I acted on this presentiment, and still do after over 30 years, and still cherish and nurture my old family. What you sow you reap, and I make a self-fulfilling prophecy for myself. One race day, hyped up in the loft, I saw an image in my mind's eye of the gaypied hen returning at great speed. Moments later, I looked up to the sun. There she was to win the race, and she glowed red.

I accept the mystical and supernatural elements of life, and have seen and met unusual men and events as far out as the Himalayas. Take a walk on the wild side, taste life on the edge. It may enrich your world, and the most profound moments in the sport are a little unworldly and mystical.

DREAMS

Why do we have them, how are they created, and what is the significance of lucid dreaming – conscious observation of a dream as it takes place? How can daily external stimuli impact on the formation of a sleep dream? What is the link between a daydream and creativity, and personality type? Can dreams be predictive of future external events? Are dreams from a subconscious part of the psyche? Let's talk about dreams, and how they impact on our psychology in the individual and society.

PRESCRIBED PSYCHOACTIVE DRUGS

Millions take mind-altering psychotropic drugs. I have known people who trick the GP and manipulate the dosage for various effects on mood and behaviours. This interests me, since the chemicals may act like certain street narcotics. The impact of legal and illegal mind/personality drugs on global humanity is enormous, and permeates every echelon of social activity.

I note that a great deal of art/poetry and music is created under the influence of drugs, particularly of a psychedelic, mystical and original nature. I find these tendencies fascinating in terms of insights, perceptions and how they impact on our understanding of psychology. The area of mental illness and psychosis as perceived by society and psychiatry is fascinating to me, and a very deep, fluid and subjective area that defies dogma and absolute understanding – a complex mind is a vast reservoir of depth. Some prescribed drugs may mask or induce madness – how potent is that?

ACADEMIC UNDERACHIEVEMENT IN HIGH IQ ADULTS

Within the individual person, I feel it is important to recognise a high IQ or gifted nature, so that these traits can be nurtured, developed and expressed in life. People need an outward expression of themselves in an acceptable academic or creative form, either in writing/art or other modes of expression. I find that my self-esteem rises with the degree of originality that I muster in my articles and poetry, most of which are published, as it gives external reinforcement of the inner, intellectual and spiritual man. Without this self-enhancing stimulation, I may feel withdrawn and depressed. I feel this is very appropriate with people who may suffer certain problems with say autism/schizophrenia or depression where morbidity may be a consequence of a lack of academic stimulation, development and expression. We should mentor the needy in these areas, perhaps through MENSA?

WHAT IS GREAT LITERATURE?

As a writer/poet/journalist I see no absolute human definition of great literature. It can be asserted by individuals or groups at any time, which I interpret as a subjective process, even after the selection criteria are defined in an apparently objective way. In accord with my own psyche I liked Kafka's Metamorphosis, and the Auguries of Innocence and the Songs of Experience by William Blake. The collective works of C G Jung changed my life and a priori are great. I prefer work which has a profound effect on the inner self, helping you to grow as an individual from within. I base all my work on existential personal experience and look for unique figures of speech. I like works which challenge the accepted conventions of the day, leaving creative and novel traces behind in pursuit of personal truth that resonates from deep within.

WOMAN CRYING

Her dark, soulful eyes are the mirror of sultry sexuality, perfected by centuries of womanhood, the hair, a glossy glow of raven plumes frames a face of ethereal and delicate beauty. The full and sensuous lips move in synchrony with the soft sounds of a lady fired by the passions of a soul enriched by earthy encounters with men. Yet what captivates me most is a single tear as it falls down her flushing cheek. Running deep from inner melancholy, it triggers a wonderful feeling of cruel beauty, and encapsulates pure emotion within and without.

LIFE AFTER DEATH

The future of the physical form is easy to understand, as the body breaks down into its inner components, eg atoms and molecules, and may make a contribution to other life forms or physical structures, being recycled in nature. Now the inner spirit of man can be projected to be perceived outside the body – this can be a fact, well documented, and I have had two such personal experiences – details can be provided. This relatively common phenomenon raises the question as to the possible continued existence of the spirit after so-called death, with a bearing on concepts of god, the brain and immortality.

BELIEF IN THE PARANORMAL

The only belief system with any great credibility to me is the one I have evolved myself from personal experience, which smacks of truth and reality; it serves me well. The so-called paranormal has enriched my life, around the world. For example a seer in Delhi read the one word that had lodged in my conscious mind, and my Jack Russell terrier, Freddie, behaved in response to some of my planned intentions as I quietly thought them through from a still and meditative state. Jean and I often share a sort of joint, collective mental state of communication, which underpins the conscious ego. The totality of human and scientific knowledge and awareness skims the surface of absolute reality, which may not be known even by the mystic or metaphysical, human philosopher.

THE CONCEPT OF THE EVOLUTION OF THE UNIVERSE

It may depend on our perception as to whether evolution has taken place or not, and conventional theories on the Big Bang proposition, science, cosmology, philosophy and other human-based activities of consciousness. It is simple to accept the notion that the universe just is, and its essence is beyond our comprehension. Do we not project our belief and bias on to external phenomena, assuming they exist? In my mind's eye it may be pertinent via introspection to examine the evolution of the individual and our own ego, or self-consciousness. This concept may baffle you in its complexity and may smack of the metaphysics of mysticism, but it is the quintessence of my work as a poet. It may be of interest for you to know that I graduated in science, yet studied humanities, the arts and the occult. I was also a member of the psychedelic subculture, a world traveller and lived in the Himalaya. My own beliefs as part of my gift are personal to me, and in that existential sense are unique. They suit me fine. They may appear to be egoist or solipsistic, yet they are real. I enjoyed writing this.

MYSTIC MARATHON MAN

A life with birds of great stamina and endurance is mind enhancing. In the setting sun as the twilight bats take out innocent moths and the sky is blackened by roosting crows, the arrival of a bird from foreign lands is a haunting and beautiful experience. The tension has risen within as the evening is suffused by wistful melancholy. A true fancier finds himself in the witching hour with the rising moon, and the warm summer stillness. With senses sharpened by an electric brain, to the sweet sounds of the orchestra of nature, as a ghost owl floats by on silent ethereal wings, you are absorbed in soulful mysticism into the womb of nature. Men have sought this euphoria since the very first primordial race.

AQABA

The craggy herdsman seated alone

Beckoned me to loin him there,

Sharing the cold water from a silver jug,

Offering chicken split fresh from the sizzling bird.

Sharing moments of rare connection

Yet not a word spoken

The note he gave me bore his name,

A proud, benign Arab herdsman.

THE YETI

I live on snow-clad peaks

One of nature's freaks

Not just a showman

I am the abominable snowman

Dwelling in the mountains

I drink from streams and fountains

Now I can drive you loco

As you try to take my photo.

I am a will o' the wisp

You want to see me clear and crisp

I dwell within the shallows

Behind rocks, stones and shadows

To haunt you with a history

Of folklore, time and mystery.

THE LUCID PROFESSOR

I lecture on global trips with lofty manuscripts,

My papers pass the censors, Prometheus, Giga and MENSAs

An oddball in a team of us, the unworldly higher genius.

LOVE

Love has a human face

It is fuelled by lust, beauty and desire,

Formed from a primal craving,

It can transcend all

Dwelling in emotion and yearning

And at the centre of art, music and poetry

Cements the sea of humanity

And gives birth to us all.

MY CONCEPT OF KNOWLEDGE
AND THE ABSOLUTE

There are people who believe that the totality of information apparently revealed by

the scientific method is a representation of reality. As an idealist, l can accept those who believe in what science has to offer, since on a certain level of consciousness this can be regarded as reality.

When l was in my twenties I became aware that the quintessence of science was centred on the collective consciousness of science, and throughout historical time in the light of the existence of many other sentient life forms on Planet Earth that also may exist or have existed in the universe throughout time, and may exist in the future; I came to realise that humans only experience a limited perception of knowledge or anything else within the cosmos.

My concept of God, ie the absolute, is the perception or subjective

experience of everything that it is possible for any life form in the
universe to know by any life form within the universe, I through
all space and time, and includes any concept of God and all words
and life.

IT IS SO SIMPLE

Genius and madness?

What are these strangers, these

faces of the diamond of abnormality?

They are but notions, expressions

Of the main ebb and flow

That cast a shadow and shed light

On the outer realms of consciousness.

They are the sword of difference,

The cutting edge of cultural history

That springs out of the eccentric

into the main stream.

We label them, pursue them with a relish,

Yet we fall short of true understanding

Unless of course we are cursed and blessed with these

Magic phantoms of the mind.

POEM FOR JEAN

You saved me from the shadows of hell,

And plucked me from the arms of insanity

Now I lie naked, warmed by your ethereal glow.

You are my beginning and my end,

A loving light in the eternal sea of love,

We are but one soul,

An unbreakable fusion into infinity, space and time;

Words can but hint at the wondrous place we now share.

FREEDOM

A bird flies from behind the sun

It hovers in the eye of the wind

Lighting up the sky with sweet music.

The glistening raindrop sheds from my face,

I feel the joy and flow of life

At one with the elements

Ego surrendered to the warm embrace of nature

Not a man, but part of the great cosmic whole

Moments of pure perfection and being.

HUMAN KINDNESS

Now that you're famous

Rich and clever

Who knows the message on sensitive whiskers?

Money lasting forever

The being within the tiny form

just takes time to reflect

Taking its place on Planet Earth

And makes sure you connect

Seductress of the stealthy cat

From the annals of your mind

Picked off by the ghostly owl.

See what you can find

And lured by chocolate into the mortal trap

Listen to the voice of reason;

Yet we love and defend these creatures

Find a little understanding

From ancient time into eternity

Because human kindness is overflowing

And I think it's going to rain today.

GOD

We search for completeness, the cosmic creator.

Our imagination fashions a grand design,

Gives meaning to our earthly

Suffering and confusion.

We build temples, institutions, think

Our way into faith and belief,

Take our place above the beast

Spiritual eternity is the prize,

Yet God is real, God is all.

His cosmic completeness

Reflects the face of pure humanity.

THE DWARF

I am the little dwarf

Wish I could grow and morph

Very small and insignificant

My ego bold, magnificent

In my imagination

I am the world of fascination

Within my soul I am a lionheart

Leader of me right from the start

I tower above the world with finality

Impress them all, a personality.

THE SELF

Take me on a kaleidoscopic journey

To the centre of consciousness,

To the far reaches of outer and inner space,

To trace the footsteps of primordial man.

Be at one with the cosmic whole,

Take warmth from imagination's fire,

Bask in the glory of uniqueness

Marvel at the divine beauty of the diamond, the lotus,

The archetype of archetypes.

Leave a footprint in the sands of time.

THE COSMOS

The cosmos embraces our delusions that it can be known,

The totality of science takes a minuscule place in the great web,

All is one, one is all and thus it will be into space, time, infinity.

Beyond the word science, God is The immensity of ultimate reality.

With vain delusion man seeks to know the unknowable,

Since all he sees is his own reflection.

THE MYSTIC MAN

The mystic man, his spirit brim full of truth,

Has pierced the deceptions of conscious reason

Penetrated the secrets of human existence

And found himself united with the whole.

With wisdom profound and self-secured

He takes his eternal place within the bosom

Of the cosmic sphere

Strange to the West and maligned by some

He tastes the sweet nectar of life's experience.

WATER

The highest good is like water

It dwells in places that men despise

Thus it approaches the Tao,

Taking life and birth

To the niches of the sea

Feeds us, fuels us with nature's elixir.

A single drop falls from my skin

To remind me that l am alive today.

THE PSYCHIC

The psychic sees beyond the "normal"

Making sense of fleeting moments, of possibilities

Bringing reality to the nebulous and the vague,

Clearing a path into the future.

Eyes illumined, he pierces the shadows

And shines a torch of truth and of reality.

His voice is heard by those who know.

HELL

Let us take a journey into despair
To a place where the mind is void
Taste the fiery heat of insanity,
Fly on the wings of delusion
Find solace in a scrum
Be consumed by unconscious force
Lose ourselves in the empty sea of humanity,
Be consumed by the dark shadow
Never to return to the light of day.

HEAVEN

Heaven is a flight on the wings of euphoria,
It is sweet embrace by the arms of ecstasy
Seduction by the light of the golden temple
Mystic realisation of selfhood
A pure essence of being beyond the word, the God, the world.
It dwells in purity, at the core of beauty
The lover's sigh, wings of the butterfly
Nectar of the senses.

PARADISE

I float away without a care
on wispy wings from my armchair
It is a reality all its own
a little dream to a world unknown,
where eagles soar across the sky
and butterflies flit on emerald wings.

The hand of man has long been gone
to leave behind the moon and sun
As I float upon an ethereal cloud
spirit unleashed to make me proud
to be born again in purist form
Beyond the clod the earthly form
Not closing my eyes for me to see
This lovely feeling – reality.
The paradise bird flies into view
to complete the picture for the chosen few.

WHEN THE LIGHT GOES OUT

My eyes are dim, my spirit candle flickers from inside the inner void
the light of day and truth is nebulous and cloaked by a dark shadow.
I am in the cycle once more, with hope and faith to restore
losing track of time, no more feelings so sublime.
In the mirror I stare, a cross my burden to bear
The brain in so much pain, trauma beyond repair.
I need a little push
of happy sweetest rush
to make me whole again
To sing my song, a sweet refrain.
I must ignite the flame
and get back on my feet again.

CLOUDS

My head floats gently in cotton wool clouds

My little dream spells out loud my sweet escape

from reality harsh, the whispering sands, the woods, the marsh

Cumuli of freedom are the nectar of my soul

they give me strength and make me whole

My wondrous dream, a beautiful dance

is the heart of my romance

as my spirit soars, an enchanted lark

that soars up to the pale blue sky

a symbol of beauty in the finest eye.

I know my place among the stars

A lofty spirit ascends to Mars

to leave the earth beneath my feet

the clay, the clod of men that speak

of worldly thoughts, material things

No more the bird that enchants and sings.

SIX STRINGS

Sweet sounds, pure and lovely to my ears, emanate from the soul
and mind of a hero. The guitar is a medium that tunes into the spirit
of the gifted who choose to pluck its heart. I feel the waves wash over
my spirit, leaving it pure and refined. It is the chord of beauty and of
truth. An echo is heard at the core of the cosmos.

REBIRTH: THE SPIRIT MORPH

Aloof, withdrawn, alone, in a dream, a spirit unfurled, my sensitive
crab of a person reacted to a vibrant and powerful sensory world.
The invasive influence of people and objects created an abstract and
intellectual being, a complex state of social isolation. This persona
would find reward and solace in a labyrinth of books and academia.
The gradual evolution with travel and the confidence of maturity
saw the rush of inner awakening, as the spirit morphed into an
ethereal human butterfly. This is the completion of my human
metamorphosis into the poet of now.

ALL THE GREAT CHARACTERS MUST DIE

Great beings, they fly on the wings of originality and freedom

Eccentric, off centre and singular, ploughing a furrow of rich earth,

for fellow man to enjoy the fruits of their creative impulse

in letters, in art, in print.

Genius linked to madness, they bask in the sunshine

on the edge of life itself.

Senses heightened, they dare to be different in a euphoric lust for life.

Some may press upon the popular consciousness of acceptability. No
longer alone in a cell, an enigma, they are celebrated and at the
heartbeat of shallow fame.

Yet as the night stars twinkle

and the sun goes down

they will wither and die

and their dust will be borne on the winds of time.

BAD LOVE

In naive innocence, and in her flame of desire,

she absorbed me, trapped in an impossible web of pain, of anguish,

fuelled by hopeless intoxication.

Her feminine fire reached the inner core of my childish vulnerability.

The helpless tension born of impending heartbreak,

the fragmented ego, as the future closed in,

the final curtain on an ill-prepared odyssey

into the seat of tortured emotions

And now in sombre reflection,

and as a hideous compensation

by emerging spirituality,

I still look with favour on womankind,

despite the trauma of bad love.

CHEERFUL TODAY

Some may say I'm sanguine today, my cheeks are all rosy,

flushed warm and bright as a posy.

Awakened from my stupor full of charm and good humour.

Life never dull, my little glass is full of warmth and understanding

My happiness strong and commanding.

Feeling jovial, slick and hip, I must not let myself slide and slip.

INDUCING THE MYSTICAL

It may well be that we have a genetically-based propensity towards
experiencing the mystical. However, from my own subjective
viewpoint, let me indulge you in a few thoughts.

If you are as we say "gifted", you may be very aroused by external stimuli. These may be musical or any "objects" which flood the senses, eg a thunderstorm, a rainbow, a monsoon, a crowd. In India, a mountain peak, like Annapurna, Nepal. In my worldly travels in Europe, Africa, America and Asia, I have sometimes been awestruck. Here you may feel a small yet beautifully significant part of the whole with a distinct loss of ego/identity.

We know that mystical experiences can be induced by sexual arousal, narcotics or psychotropic drugs. Now these may have deep effects on your psychic awareness and perception.

What certainly works for me is to detach my conscious mind from what is thought as "external" reality. This is easy, with quiet concentration, and I confess to this absent-minded activity. The pure rush of being you may experience under this self-induced hypnotic state – a lovely feeling like ecstasy – is indeed described as mystical. A pure and uncluttered feeling state.

Be careful who you tell – they will think you are mad!

A SNOWMAN'S DREAM

The new day dawns, it's Christmas morn

I find I'm flying across the sky

On my way to you, and why?

To scatter snowflakes on the tree

The wondrous star, a celebrity.

I bring you joy, and season's wonder

Magic to all asunder

A little boy stirs within his soul

To glimpse my lovely snowclad whole

Each person a life less tragic

Is now in raptures with my magic.

FREEDOM

A bird flies from behind the sun

It hovers in the eye of the wind

Lighting up the sky with sweet music

The glistening raindrop rolls from my face

I feel the joy and flow of life

At one with the elements

Ego surrendered to the warm embrace of nature

Not a man, but part of the great cosmic whole

Moments of pure perfection and being.

LOVE

Love has a human face

It is fuelled by lust, beauty and desire

Formed from a primal craving

It can transcend all

Dwelling emotion and meaning

And at the centre of art, music and poetry

Cements the sea of humanity

And gives birth to us all.

THE SELF

Take me on a kaleidoscopic journey

To the centre of consciousness

To the far reaches of outer and inner space

To trace footsteps of primordial man

Be at one with the cosmic whole

Take warmth from imagination's fire

Bask in the glory of uniqueness

Marvel at the divine beauty of the diamond, the lotus,

the archetype of archetypes.

Leave a footprint in the sands of time.

GENIUS AND MADNESS?

What are these strangers,

these facets of the diamond of abnormality?

They are but notions, expressions of the main ebb and flow

that cast a shadow and shed light

In the outer realms of consciousness.

They are the sword of difference

The cutting edge of cultural history

That spring out of the eccentric into the mainstream norm.

We label them, pursue them with a relish,

yet we fall short of true understanding

Unless of course we are cursed and blessed

With these magic phantoms of the wind.

MODERN TIMES

Retirement heralded my metamorphosis from the humble rigours of
a local authority gardener into a MENSA poet, writer and serious
contributor to the pigeon racing culture via the media of published
interviews with the alumni, features and a host of serious articles. I
belong to 13 special interest groups of MENSA and aim to publish in
all the journals. For a few years I enjoyed creating features for the
Kew Guild Journal. My garden, a honeypot for bees and butterflies,
is a fusion of the wild and cottage garden styles. I contemplate the
many cultivars of narcissi in the collection and have counted 14
species of butterfly on the buddleia. Not predominantly tidy, it is a
vibrant little ecosystem, a living testimony to my love of nature and

aesthetic sensibility. The poppies bloom in rich and vibrant profusion, the goldfinches continue to charm, and birds eke out their short lives on the feeding tables in great variety. In my creative writing I express my love of ideas, images and nature, and encapsulate the essence of my colourful, diverse and original experiences of a life which has vibrated with the notes of rich complexity. There is a zen-like purity and simple spirituality to all things.

II

The Human Condition

HUMAN CONSCIOUSNESS AND ABSOLUTE KNOWLEDGE

It would appear that some interactive knowledge about the external world is available to certain minds. Much as I try, and although I have a penetrating perception of my inner, psychic man, I know I fall short of attaining total, absolute knowledge of anything, especially in the outer sphere of things, nature, humans and inanimate objects.

I have experienced mystical feelings, when a sense of unity of the inner being with all is felt, a lovely human experience. If we could assemble, unite and harness the total consciousness of humanity that has existed throughout time, I feel that the essence or absolute reality of anything would not be known – it is not in the nature of man to be omniscient, omnipotent or omnipresent. Scientists and believers may consider this to avoid false beliefs, bias and dogma which can hinder the journey to light and truth as sought by consciousness.

CONSCIOUSNESS AND MYSTICAL FEELINGS

Having experienced altered and higher states of being, the most powerful have been feelings of sublime purpose and connection with life, accompanied by great lucidity, awe and euphoria. In human terms this can be labelled as a mystical state, and although unique in the individual it is not unusual after meditation, drug use or sex, or in the presence of the raw power of nature, eg a hurricane, a thunderstorm or a sunrise. It can be life-changing and enhancing, and it is the engine room of my poetry and philosophy and essential being. Many write and speak of conceptual/intellectual mysticism, yet it is a part of the differentiation of my insights and psyche.

A JOINT CONSCIOUSNESS?

We perhaps think that we are singular and unique individuals, part of a collective whole called humanity. Notions of individual, rational and ego-led consciousness may reinforce this view. My experiences as perceived in the presence of my wife, and out in the wilderness of nature, make me aware of some unity of thought and being, which perhaps indicates a link between our physical, functioning brains in a resulting joint consciousness. To my mind's eye this may have an impact on ideas of identity, the self and the group identity, and its relevance to philosophy and psychology in our modern thinking about ourselves in relation to the bigger spheres of society, nature and the cosmos. It may have a bearing on the roles we play and our social purpose and responsibilities, do you feel?

THE MEANING OF LIFE

A particle in space of the human race

within the cosmos I ponder my place

In the world I find with my tiny mind

a place I must in my spirit trust.

The meaning of without and within

Is formed from pain and sin

A mind that glows from the brain, that flows

In words of truth and meaning

At the world I stare without a care

As the emergent spirit morphs and grows its wonders to bestow

A life so rich I am born full of truth and meaning

My journey is now complete, a leap of faith in the hands of fate.

BANGING YOUR OWN DRUM

I sing my song, play my tune, alone inside my room.

Others' beliefs I do not share, of gods, of politics I despair.

A single chord I play, the one note here to stay,

that resonates deep within my mind and heart and worldly sin.

Why conform to conventional norm

when my mind can create a storm

in words, in print, the dreams of men

that emerge from deep within.

I flow with the tide, on the wind I ride,

to the moon and Mars, the sun and the stars.

I know my place in the pulse of life, and the final outcome

is to bang on my drum.

DARK WEB

Men on the stage of life attempt a subtle balancing act, poised on complex and subtle strands as they act out the parts that the web of society imposes on them. Prisoners of the demands and roles, afloat in a sea of convention and conformity, yet yearning for the sweet rush of freedom. Artists and poets may feel the pulse of originality, an expression of the true nature, of existential reality, nurture and sustenance as purist beauty feeds impoverished souls. Genius is the reward for gifted souls who pursue a dream with a fervour and a passion that gives true meaning and value to humanity. So shed the cloak, discard the mask, escape the dark web of personal nothingness.

THE PRISONER

The conscious eye, observing and ever alert to the inner self, is critical, punitive and watchful that kind feelings should be liberated, setting the spirit free. Blessed am l that this is transient torture, a symptom of a disordered brain. ln sanguine moments insights coloured by beauty linger to create lofty and ethereal images that burst into print. I know the value of the beautiful mind, as now I am being liberated, as the prisoner escapes from the cauldron, the purgatory of the unconscious psyche. The self is the unity from the whirlpool of inner complexity, as l touch back to reality.

THE NATURE OF GENIUS

It is the fire-blade of intuition, the sword of creativity, from behind the mask of originality.

A fluid form, it inhabits the hearts and minds of intellectuals and artists who change the landscape of popular and esoteric consciousness.

Shrouded in mystery and reverence for its absorbing power, it vibrates on the chord of notes, as unique perceptions by individuals, yet is collectively described as genius.

Shallow attempts are made to pierce its depths when we feel and sense fleeting shadows of the abyss, since it is a journey and an expression of humanity itself.

Who were the creators of The Scream, the Songs of Innocence,

Who was man behind the common perception of Einstein?

It is exciting in the realisation that we know when it is encountered.

A SOLITARY MAN

I am a solitary man, doing what I can

To make sense of this life's span

The babes are born of one accord, and set out on the journey of life.

All the people I have known throughout the world are but shadows of the unknown.

They are but ships that pass in the night, obscured from sight,

and to meet one we really know feeds the inner glow.

In one seminal moment we may share moments of communion and truth, yet as time flashes by I know that I am a solitary man.

It is enough to know from a spiritual glow

that I have done what no other can.

DEATH

In the darkest shadows of the psyche

Lurks the ultimate reality of man,

Power so absolute, so total without escape,

Waiting to take us to eternity

To the void, to the centre of its core

And when our earthly quest is done,

Our dust and atoms will make it whole.

From the moment of our birth

Death has us in its mighty grip.

COSMIC JOURNEYMAN

I am the Cosmic King,

on the earth and born to sing.

I probe the questions of life and death,

from the brain and mind at my behest.

A spiritual journey I have begun,

of inner space and so much fun,

to ponder all from near and far,

the babbling brook, the shooting star.

One day I sense the light may fade,

my moon, my sun to fall in shade,

as I earn my place in the fallen leaves,

no more to shine and be perceived

by those who light the fires of truth

of the cosmic man, the mindful sleuth.

THE ZONE

Aloof, detached in my little world of possibilities, I am cocooned in cotton wool.

My beautiful retreat smacks of reality to me, knows only the boundaries of a soul and imagination liberated by fancy ignited by a fiery brain.

The outer world, a shock to the senses, brings me back from the brink of madness, the edge of darkness, and the demons of the twilight world, at the core of man.

We poets know the gift of delicate images that flow from deep within the labyrinth, the whirlpool of the mind.

My personal zen is the home of reality and truth, pure and free of sensation, a womb of pure feeling.

DIE ANOTHER DAY

We live in hope, a worldly theme, to fulfil our inner dream

The great questions remain unanswered, secret, nebulous, on our long journey to the dawning of sunlight in our spiritual morning.

Warm breeze on my face brings a diamond to my eye, the eagle that soars in the heavenly sky.

I float along on wings of time my little world so sweet and sublime.

If I made a choice to leave or stay I know I would die another day.

The pulse of life is so sweet, an inner life yet to complete

another silken strand in the complex web of life on Earth.

SWEET REFLECTIONS

I am the shimmer on the waters of time, the beauty of words that rhyme.

A twinkling star I find in the essence of my mind.

Shooting stars are who we are, a beautiful pulsar. We are seekers of ethereal people, that sense and feel noble and lovely things, from the imagination that springs into life, to give form and meaning to the flowers that grow and the blooms that glow in the gardens of my mind.

THE CYCLONE OF MY MIND

I feel a stirring in the deep dark whirlpool within. It is the inner voice that bubbles and gurgles from beneath the complex of my mind. Pure and simple, and the ghost of truth, she tells me all I need to know of the world that lurks below. The flames may fan and the fires glow, more lovely feelings to bestow, within a hungry mind that seeks sanity and truth, when the whole world is but chaos. In the gardens of my head, the flowers grow, in waves of gold, red and blue, each and every hue. I close my eyes, shut down the world and dream of the paradise that grows in the cyclone of my mind.

CHASM OF THE UNKNOWN

Let us take a trip deep into the mind of man, a penetrating ultrascan. Beyond science, the fusion of religion and conclusion, we may sense the void, a dark world of truth. Beyond the shallow sea of humanity, defying all sense of reality, it invites and tantalises the mad and queer in the province of the seer. If you encounter this world, is it possible to return from the chasm of the unknown. I have been on this journey, and the spirit has morphed, evolved and is reborn into the light of day.

THE SURVIVAL INSTINCT

The drive to survive in man and other species can be very profound. In my experience it is the primary instinct and may galvanise the mind and senses. If you put people under pressure, the outer veneer produced by education and socialisation will fall away, leaving a raw, powerful and primal state of being. Out on the edge in Afghanistan, in wilderness and other scenarios where survival skills are needed, I have felt its compelling presence. It can also be felt in the naked jungle of a competitive workplace, particularly in a hierarchy where bullies prevail. Concentration camp survivors speak of an acute and selfish need that prevails over any other influence. I feel that behind the mask of collective society, beyond the dynamics of a group, every human being is an individual. I sense it, feel it and perceive it, and believe that this survival impetus pervades many lifeforms.

CONSCIOUSNESS AND THE CREATIVE PROCESS

The nature of the inner being of man and how it is expressed in creative forms fascinates me. In my own experience, my mind becomes like a conduit for the poem or article to take shape and morph from within in a completed verbal form. When relaxed, reflective and in the zone, the pilot of the mind shapes the ideas and imagery that pop up into conscious view from beneath the usual level of awareness. Great feelings of satisfaction accompany the process, or catharsis and liberation. I can understand Sartre in his Being and Nothingness, and the essence of Zen. The feelings generated are experienced as pure and simple and have the ring of personal truth to them. I realise the subjective, individual character of the process, yet it becomes objectified in print.

EGOALTRUISM

The practice of assisting others in some way by your own conscious efforts fascinates me. With positive influence it is nice to bring benefit to other people in a form of human symbiosis. I like the principle, power and integrity that it may manifest. It seems to be motivated by a degree of compassion and perhaps conscious spirituality. In my creative articles, I sense a positive contribution to my interests and to others. The feeling that is generated by this activity seems very preferable to waging war, as an illustration of power led egos. Perhaps we can enter into a psychological analysis of this personality trait?

THE EVOLUTION OF RELIGIOUS CONSCIOUSNESS SINCE PRIMORDIAL MAN

In humanity, there are many godheads and belief systems. A cosmic, supernatural power may be possible, although I have no tangible evidence of this omnipotent entity. On an intuitive level, I feel that all the belief systems and gods have been developed and evolved by man in response to our own psyche and the external world in which we live. My spirit lies within me, although I feel a deep connection with nature, and can conceive how the faithful have created institutions to reflect the human condition. The cosmos is so large that the possibility exists of other life forms with belief systems as part of their culture. My extensive travels to the roof of the world, and on the edge of survival, have strengthened my inner belief in myself as a separate entity, yet connected to the cosmos-it is all I need. The essence of truth is personal INSIGHT.

DEFINING HUMAN CONSCIOUSNESS

Psychologists, intellectuals, poets, artists and philosophers try to capture the essence of consciousness and make it tangible. It can be an attempt to verbalise and objectify what can be spiritual and ethereal. The brain is a physical organ that can be dissected, photographed and studied, yet what is the real nature of the brain/mind connection? My consciousness feels like a non-physical entity to me. I like it that way, as some of my poetry and thoughts hint at shadow and mystery. To me the great questions relating to the microcosm and the macrocosm remain unanswered by humanity, in an absolute sense. This apparent fact of life fascinates me as we can delude ourselves with the idea of omniscience. I feel that the most profound thoughts of man, hint at the well of being within.

THE THIRD EYE

I perceive this, from my own introspective observations of the psyche to be insight, acumen and foresight. These traits generated by the brain can be classed as the intuitive function of the inner man. A still, small voice may appear, which I obey as it has the ring of true perception. I make most of my life decisions using judgements from the inner man, with the clarity of instant perception. With sensory experiences in wilderness, and travels to the roof of the world, including facing danger in Afghanistan and Pakistan, where raw instinct was the survival tool, I trust the quality of the eye which operates at a deeper level than the rational, logical and intellectual function. It raises questions of self-knowledge and other psychological entities. I find that many people are out of touch and some are detached from their spiritual nature, which is fundamental to a healthy psyche.

JUDGEMENTS MADE ON MENTAL ILLNESS DIAGNOSIS

I feel that psychiatrists are assisted in their decisions in the light of personal judgements in relation to the collective knowledge of the times. A person presenting themselves may act out or accentuate all manner of personality traits, on which the doctor will make subjective decisions. The power of this process can change the lives of individuals. A change in our perceptions of Peter Sutcliffe highlights the complexities involved. Can we really fathom the inner complexity of the psyche of a human being, or do we tend to make superficial judgements on the external cues perceived from the person?

My intuitive perception informs me that the whole process is very deep and complex and may lead to variable decisions depending on the nature of all the players on the stage. A major question remains – what are the perceived natures of mental illness and mental health? This can be examined from many perspectives, eg psychological, philosophical, legal and from poetry, literature and the arts. Please discuss.

MAD WITH POWER

They come and go, men, women of today and tomorrow, and oh what sorrow they bring in the paranoia which is their thing.

With charm, con, and chicanery they worship in the art of slavery, where people are mere projections of a distorted ego.

They are intoxicated by a grand delusion of themselves, bringing subservience and obedience to the faithful. Heads of State start as masters of their fate, until the sting of reality and truth is felt, when the illusion of lies is rumbled and they fall silently to earth. Perhaps you recognise the monster within at the heart of political spin?

BRAINS IN UNISON

I have observed people's personalities, eg in couples responding in unison between themselves and to external stimuli. Their thoughts or verbalised responses seem to echo each other, almost as one joint consciousness. This raises issues of the possibility of brains and minds acting in synchrony, at a deeper level than just empathy.

How do we think the process works? How does it affect the concept of individual mind, consciousness and collective consciousness and how they impact on personal identity? Can we point to any research into these factors, and the perception and nature of being human and the idea of reality?

It may bring into play telepathy, yet I feel we can take it much further than that. What do you think on a psychological and philosophical level?

THE MOTHER OF HUMAN CONSCIOUSNESS

The inner self can be conceived as a little world within a bigger world, or a microcosm within the macrocosm. Be it the complexities of thought, belief, emotions and the total psyche from which external cultural forms generate, as architecture, art and literature, they are all created by the brain. This is my personal insight, and takes on an introspective perspective, rather than believing we are at the total mercy of cosmic powers, gods or other external forces. In fact our psychology, our physicality as individuals and humanity as a whole are parts of a unified cosmos. This intuitive perception places our brains at the centre and heart of consciousness, and is how we perceive and make sense of what we call reality in an internal and external sense. This then, is my personal understanding of the brain/mind synthesis applicable to myself, and perhaps others. I am content with it, and interested to see the personal responses of others from a human perspective of thought and belief.

MAN AND HIS PLACE IN NATURE

As living beings, humanity shares the planet with a myriad of other lifeforms. These in the grand scale of the cosmos can be perceived as one united entity of life on Planet Earth. Each creature has a role to play, and is significant in the total web of earthly existence. I believe we have an individual responsibility to nurture and treasure the vast yet declining living resources we share with countless species-from the tiniest microbe to the largest elephant. The practical essence will be understanding of conservation needs on a global level. I would like to see a rise in spiritual beliefs from within, and generated by nature, and active education of the naïve and greedy to reverse the trends of environmental pollution. The ideals are lofty and transcendent, yet the practical needs in reality are onerous and pressing.

THE UGLY FACE OF CAPITALISM

Individuals and institutions make a god out of the dreams, hopes and aspirations of the many – the accumulation of money. Avarice and greed are motivational forces and desires of needy egos, who formulate strategies as a guise for con and corruption, to create wealth and generate power, to forge a self-conscious identity.

Having found a degree of inner spirituality in my long, complex and rich life and a shrewd and perceptive eye for genuine truth, I can spot the phoney mask of many career and power-driven authority figures who pretend to be pillars of society, yet evade the truth or essence of an objective. Well-versed in rhetoric, they spin webs of charm and chicanery.

Having travelled the world, I can spot these chancers in the cauldron of capitalist society. The genuine ones illuminate the popular consciousness with pure light and integrity, and it is beautiful to see. We urgently need a huge injection of belief in spiritual core values, the sanctity of the inner man, in the sea of money-orientated capitalism which is out of control and reflects an ugly face.

PHILOSOPHY AND THE MEANING OF LIFE

I have travelled around the world, studied, meditated, examined belief systems and philosophical thought processes and have made a few insights as follows. Under the influence of the cosmos and the brain/mind synthesis, humanity does not know the nature of the intrinsic reality of the cosmos.

Science, philosophy, religion and other human processes are based within the individual and collective consciousness of man, and within the limits of language and consciousness. In the vastness of the cosmic space-time continuum, a supernatural omniscient entity may exist, and I am happy with the concept that it does or does not. In my mind I am equal to any human on earth, yet the cosmos is a larger entity than my ego which is part of it.

Humans, and possibly other sentient lifeforms, can inject any meaning they like into the mutable perception of an external world and all without dogma are relevant to the individual being. To my mind's eye we are on Planet Earth to exist and live out a lifecycle and discover the inner man or spiritual aspect -ourselves. I require no further meaning or understanding than this rather solipsistic insight. Philosophy is a nice little teaser, yet we are all less than specks of dust, mere minnows in what is in here and out there-in the last analysis I am without care.

IS MINDFULNESS GOOD FOR YOU?

As a reflective, poetic and deeply philosophical person, I work from the inner nature of my mind. As an introverted thinker, it becomes a pure way of being. I accept the Eastern influence of Taoism and Buddhism as tools of meditation. I see my mind as a microcosm led by the ego or pilot, and like to access the deeper regions of its creative power. Mindfulness suits my introspective nature fine.

Be careful what you tap into in conscious meditation, as it is a trip into the inner nature of the self, where you may encounter shadow and darkness before spiritual light. It is a sweet departure from materialism and the money god, charmed by nice music, good art and free nature.

III

Musings on the natural world

THE BOYS' ADVENTURE TALE

When I was young there was so much fun to be had

in the woods by the lake, I was far from sad

Hunting high and low for the fox, the deer and his doe.

My world was strange and insular, in mountains, forests and peninsula

As each pulse of freedom was born on the wings of adventure.

At one with the outside world, every nuance unfurled in a time of make believe.

What wonders to perceive in the song thrush, finch and grebe.

The inviting, perfect nest was a wonderfest, a lasting image of a youth well spent in the timeless memories of yesterday

When I was young, in pure naïve innocence.

THE COUNTRY BOY

I love to be where the wild goose flies across lonely skies

Morning mist and the sparkling dew

in fields where a simple few feel the power of the awakening sun.

The cock it crows, as the day comes alive to the orchestra of nature.

In far green pastures, pheasants preen like beauty queens,

unaware of the wily old fox

as it engages in the dance of death

to pounce on an unsuspecting vole,

whose concealment in the long grass is no more.

Far from the pulse of city man

I flow with the wind and the tide,

intoxicated by freedom.

This is my hour, it is my day at home in the heart of nature,

where the butterfly caresses the air with ethereal emerald wings

as the skylark sings one more sweet note

to all that is good and beautiful in the cradle of life.

MY LITTLE BANTY COCK

The cock that crows in the rising sun
the day begins with so much fun
His florid plumes in the courtship dance
to bring me magic and sometimes trance.
With legs of spurs my spirit stirs in beautiful wonder of this bird
He struts about the garden green, each lovely plume for all to see.
No words could capture what I feel for my little devil the banty cock.

LAST SUMMER SONG

I saw a butterfly today, on the final wings of yesterday
The fragile form, once so blessed with beauty,
lay trembling with dull and tattered wings.
I felt the metaphor as it stirred my soul from deep within.
It is the destiny of the imago to shimmer
like a jewel in the summer sun,
only to fade and die in chill, autumn melancholy.
I wish to turn back time,
to celebrate the magnificence of this glorious insect again,
and fix the memory in all eternity.
In the rise and fall of seasons long,
nature absorbs both life and death unto itself.

TWILIGHT BAT

In the soft light of the cold-hearted orb,
the horseshoe bat flies on gentle wings
an eerie silhouette in the night sky.
In the ebb and flow of mother earth,
a fluttering moth is taken by one predatory swoop
in a scene enacted in the theatre of life and death,
marking time since primordial man.

MOTH

Driven deep within, by primal instinct,

the creature is enticed to be immolated by the flame.

To cold science, it is a fact,

yet stirs the soul and imagination of men.

The light and moth are one, bound in life and death.

In the symphony and dance of nature it is truly wonderful.

THE OPIUM POPPY

Summer bees are drawn as magnets to the gentle nectar of her soft purple flowers, as she hides the dark secret of life and death.

I have smoked the pipe of dreams, and basked in sweet euphoria.

The humble flower that rests in the summer field evolves into a capsule, that is both the key to transcendence, and spiritual oneness.

The ultimate price you may pay is that she will consume your soul and eat away at the bodily form. One or two encounters with the Queen of Flowers will awaken you to her deathly majesty.

DANCING CRANE

They cavort and dance, in essence of romance

Black on white, a heavenly site, they enact a timeless ritual in the glistening sun. Each balletic posture is one showpiece in a fluid demonstration of avian ecstasy.

The sheer wonder to the human eye inspires intense contemplation and joy, as man is hard pressed to compete with these jewels of nature.

If born again I want to glide, a free spirit on the wings of the crane that dances and stirs the soul of man.

ANT

The mighty ant is a colossus, a giant of nature and a beacon of industry. Acting as one being, the ordered society is a survival model for chaotic and disharmonious man.

In the theatre of raw survival ants approach perfection, for sheer tenacity of fixed purpose. A closely-observed hierarchy forms a design and pattern of intrinsic beauty, that dominates and claims the life of a myriad of lesser beings in the inexorable drive and fight for supremacy.

Imagine a phantom world where ants as giants descend to earth to devour the flesh of man; now that would create a cosmic wave.

TIGER

In the cool rays of moonlight, a stealthy hunter lurks with primal intent. The Lord and Majesty will spill blood as the forest guards his secret.

In the web of life and the call of death, a deer is taken. A thousand voices of nature do not complain; it is the way.

The spirit of the beast can be likened to a supreme being or God. In the essence of life on Earth, the strong will prevail and take a little life in the myriad of life forms that enrich Planet Earth.

A man may look into the eye of a tiger and feel profound echoes from within his soul.

ALL THE LITTLE CREATURES

All the little creatures are one, from the lion to the ant and scorpion.

A feeling remains that fills me with wonder and awe, and needing more of the butterfly, moth and gentle sloth, of the wild geese that fly across twilight skies.

I love to see the ascending lark, the thrush that sings and the birch tree bark.

Of all the heavenly things I've seen, the paradise bird is the beauty queen.

A lion may thrill as the blood does spill, but as the eagle soars my spirit calls me back to the pure embrace of nature.

THE PEACOCK

This enchanting creature radiates exotic beauty in the essence of each brilliant blue eye spot. The fan sways and shimmers, in glistening purple and blue, kissed by the warm summer sunshine. A wondrous spectacle sharpens the senses, in a primal dance on the stage of nature.

The mere human eye struggles to capture the impression on canvas, in a scene that is the dance of love, each step a moment in time and with the power of history, encapsulated in the present.

EYE OF THE WIND

Gentle breeze, floating zephyr, the soul of nature in the palm of my hand.

Feeling so alert, larger than life, embracing the dark and lonely night.

I see the owl, the shooting stars, so high, yet I can fly right up to touch the sky.

With boundary gone, the radiant sun descends to earth and makes me one.

The pulse of life, the ebb and flow, with wonders to bestow as I part the husk

to feel the rush, the essence of things in the eye of the wind.

THE BUZZARD

A buzzard soars on thermal high

Such wildness in his piercing eye

On unsuspecting hare he will swoop, instinct is his only guide

Man with all his intellect will never match nature's stride.

PARADISE BIRD

In the jungle depths, the jewels gather and lek, the dance of diamonds and emeralds to perform. Extroverts, shamans of the avian world, they shimmer, entice and illuminate. It is an act of love, fuelled by time, and has outlived the dawn of man. The pure psychedelia of the performance, must be a pinnacle of evolution, or a mysterious act of creation, unsurpassed as a spectacle of beauty. Little wonder that men believe in other worldly Gods.

WHERE THE WILD GOOSE FLIES

Deep in estuarine wilderness, alone with the wind and tide, in sight of endless horizon, my fire was ignited. Curlew appeared in the mist, ghostly and with eerie, plaintive calls that have endured over aeons of time. Mother seals called their young in mournful cries that echoed over the vast flatlands of the saltings. Vast skeins of geese loomed large, creating an unearthly clamour as they sped across the evening sky. Men in city suits live in stark ignorance of this beauty, the soul of nature.

MY FIRST GOOSE

The lure of the Wash Wilderness overtook me, and in Sept 1969, I found myself alone on Kenzie Thorpe's houseboat. Moored on the saltings, she had been the temporary home of many a wildfowling eccentric as the rugged old Kenzie was a guide and singular wild goose man. A colourful, and most original man, his associates included Prince Charles, actor James Robinson Justice and Sir Peter Scott. As a boy I was in great company with Romany Kenzie.

For the evening flight, I hid in a narrow tidal creek in sight of the river Welland. From the eerie silence of the open seascape and saltings, I heard a skein of very early pinkfeet and called them loudly, and in hope and wonder. Freezing to the spot, I was amazed as the voices grew louder; they were winging towards my hiding place.

It was both a seminal and an awesome experience when I pulled out a gosling with the twelve-bore. It was 22nd Sept 1969 at 6.10 in the evening, and the story appeared in Shooting Times. Life gives you one chance to do what you love and enjoy, and it is not a rehearsal, it is the real thing.

THE WALNUT TREE

Branches pruned by the winds of time, she stood above the sweet meadow of my youth. A symbol of young ambition, present but not known by a simple mind, I dared to climb to the uppermost, thinning branches, intoxicated by risk. In an act that fulfilled young senses and desires, I descended, racked by anxiety to the touchdown safety of cushioning grass. And now in reflective nostalgia, the tree long gone is a symbol of my worldly and spiritual aspirations, as in my font of memories it is life itself. We all need trees to enrich and to grow in the forests of the imagination.

THE FIELDFARES HAVE LANDED

On wings of historical time, giving vibrancy to the sound of nature, they sit high up on ancient ash trees. In communion and as winged and social creatures, they descend on hedgerow fruits, bounty so freely given as if by the hand of god. It is ancient lore, beyond the understanding of man, knowledge and science. To the perceptive eye, ear tuned in to the orchestra of nature, it is a rebirth. This earthly beauty can lift the spirit into one beautiful, timeless, mystical moment.

THE SWALLOWS ARE GOING

With a warm and helping wind, out of ancient and unknown urges they attempt the epic flight of endurance to the Sahara. Young ones may linger until October in certain parts, and I recall little ones in the nests of the wash pillboxes in September. This migration is a living metaphor of man's ignorance of the essence, the subtleties and complexities of nature. The awesome nature of the feat is both elemental, romantic and inspirational. Gazing upon the little wonders I am alerted and then transfixed, and inspired to poetry. we are passengers on the planet, our transient and ephemeral existence bathed in ignorance. surely a singular swallow has the key to untold secrets

WE CALL IT SPRING

My silent contemplation of emergent life is like a time lapse of the mind.

The gentle bee in sweet harmony hums a concerto of nature, as the yellow brimstone butterfly wafts by on zephyr wings.

It is the season of buoyant optimism, when man and nature are united in transcendence.

The sublimity of its essence induces zen-like states of mindfulness, in the rich flow of the mystical experience.

Beyond the god, inside the material mask of life, is the pulse and quintessence of man himself, in the sweet rush of life on earth.

EYE OF THE WIND

Voices of nature born on the wind, exhilarating giving fire to the spirit of birds and sentient beings.

Soft ethereal whispers as spiders float through the air on silken zephyrs.

Destructive, tempestuous, branches of ancient trees, aching and bent over with the storms of time.

The wind, a pure element, giving life and taking it, with a relentless drive from the unknown. Man strains to harness its path of freedom, yet nature rules the earthly sphere.

The arrogance and delusion of humanity fails in its attempt at control, as the relentless eye of the wind prevails.

MEASURES TO ENRICH THE ECOSYSTEM IN MY GARDEN

The plants form a canopy of total groundcover in a diverse variety of native and non-native genera. The buddleia has fed many species of butterfly, with humming bird hawk moths occasional visitors. My impression border, with florid nasturtiums and papaver, is intoxicating to bumblebees and other insects. Foxes, birds and hedgehogs like the patch, and the whole area hums with the drone of insects. I avoid regimented, tidy plantings and adopt a 'let it grow' philosophy. Insecticides and herbicides are banned, and the whole ethos is bohemian and back to nature, in pure love and respect of nature. We will all take our place as dust and atoms at the culmination of our lives.

SNOW

The warmth on my face is heat generated by snowflakes that cling to my ruddy cheeks. As the ice crystals melt on my warming breath, I feel exhilarated alone in the wild, alive in earthly elements. In the sultry heat of the summer sun, I feel the power and the pull of icebound winds, which charge me with electricity.

Raw nature is the essence that created me, mind body and soul have made me whole, the whispering sands, the howling wind, and the rising tide of salty springs.

There are certain men who come alive far from the crowd and the nine till five. I am that man who found a way to sense and be intoxicated by a glorious freedom.

THE ORCHESTRA OF NATURE

My senses have been tuned by woodlands and wilderness and where wild geese flight over lonely salt marshes. The web of nature fascinates me, as does the intricate communication between different species of birds, animals and other life forms in the collective pulse of life. When a cat lurks, or a buzzard soars, there is a crescendo of sound and avoidance behaviour. This is the opiate of a glowing mind, and a rush to the senses. In the sea of life, which flows with ethereal resonance, are a myriad of characters, accents and regional variations, comprising the enigma of life itself. A life played out in the theatre of the earth colours the inner tapestry of man himself.

THE VOICE OF NATURE

The world is alive with a sea of species, and a subtle, yet evident communication and understanding between many life forms in vibrant ecosystems. Science led by humans falls short of true understanding of the theatre of life. If you sit in a wood, or snorkel in the Red Sea, or watch the waders on the Wash saltings lapped by a rising spring tide, you may feel a mystical connection, a union with it all. The conscious ego that creates a sense of 'I' may dissolve as you feel a profound sense of awe, as when I faced Annapurna in the Himalaya. Man tends to dissect and analyse the external world, of life, of nature, yet it is all one entity that includes mankind. As a man I prefer poetic and philosophical perspectives on nature and find great beauty in them.

MY LITTLE SPRING GARDEN

Many poppy seedlings – my favourites – have survived from sowing last autumn. I have 36 hyacinths coming out in 9 cultivars, which brighten up dull days. The jew's mallow is flushed with yellow, and the impression border is waking up. The lawns, growing all year, have been fertilised with Scotts' compound, and rose fertiliser is scattered all over the mixed borders.

THE WILLOW

Willow, shed your tears on the lake below,

Lend wispy leaves to the vernal glow

You stand majestic for man to see

An image of nature, a fantasy.

You keep your secrets beneath the bough

We gaze upon, and how

The wonder of nature casts its spell,

As I walk along this lonely dell.

SPRING IN THE GARDEN

I meditate on my lovely flowers each day. There are many genera and species of narcissus, tulips and iris to study and absorb colour sensations from. All are a colourful microcosm of life. My garden is monasterial, a sanctum approaching zen mindfulness. The new fence is waiting for the 10 luxurious climbers to burst forth into activity, supported by a creative mixture of native wild flowers, sweet peas, nasturtiums and gladioli underneath in eccentric profusion. My imagination has been in concert with nature since boyhood, and I continue in my hypersensitive, personal way to love the external world of life forms that are the ecosystem of my garden.

GERTRUDE THE GRASS

Nestled deep inside my luxuriant womb is the warm shelter of all the little creatures of the magic garden. I am the home of a myriad of lives that vibrate and jostle in rich and verdant green. Beneath my green leaves the game of life is played out in the secret theatre of nature. My nature is to nurture, feed and guard the mouse, the bee, the flower and the tree. And thus the seeds of existence are sown, to flower and grow in the garden where spells are cast, the sun shines and the angel sings sweet songs of innocence.

SAMMY THE SWALLOW

The free air is his universe, swooping and flitting about on a warm summer breeze. Gregarious and excitedly loquacious, he engages in the ancient language of the swallows, as they enact a brief and eventful life born of tradition and instinct. Alert to aerial predators, escaping them, avoiding them in a deathly dance that haunts the blue skies, he scoops one more fly from the summer harvest of winged morsels. And then as the days close down into autumnal darkness, he will fly on a journey of epic survival, across forest and seas, a singular endurance flight across the whispering sands of the Sahara, and once more the circle of life is complete.

WILLIE THE WORM

He inhabits the subconscious darkness of a subterranean world. Living in harmony with the little lives that are the beat and pulse of nature, he pops out to perpetuate his kind. In the earthly sphere, this urge is eternal and immortal as long as the planet exists. His urge to mate above the cast may spell doom, as the blackbird waits, poised, with murderous intentions. And so the web of life is enriched by one more silken strand, each little life form, a price to pay in the part they play in the cosmic theatre of being.

THE BUTTERFLY

Butterfly dancing before my eyes

Ethereal beauty in the skies

Eyes of peacock spread thy wings

Eternal image, my heart just sings

Live your life with grace and flair

Bring me wonder with every stare.

An image of god's spell to cast,

With fire of life so short and fast.

THE KINGFISHER

O malachite, transfix me with your emerald beauty

Surrender your lustrous reflection to the depths of the lake,

Shimmer with your colours of rainbow,

And transport my spirit into the arms of ecstasy.

THE FLY

A little fly cuts the sky

The swallow swoops, since it must die;

It matters not to you and I,

Ours is not to wonder why

And once more, Mother Nature's great wheel of life is turned.

THE EAGLE

An eagle's eye burns its path across the sun

Driven by spirit his instincts to pursue,

Horizon pierced by forceful glare,

The prey an unsuspecting mountain hare.

Man can but ponder and wonder how

This mighty bird in freedom's glow

Lights a fire in the earthly sky.

THE OWL

The owl floats by on whispering wings

A ghostly spectre tugs my heartstrings

His ears pierce the gloomy night

Seeking prey, his earthly flight.

Yet I with reason bright as day

Forever tread the earthbound clay.

THE SPIDER

A spider lies quivering on a silken strand,

His short life the epitome of silent patience

Why disturb this little soul?
His essence will be a singularity
In the great scheme of things.
This lone arachnid must take his place
In the eternal web of life and death,
And so it has been and will be;
A living microcosm in the universal whole.

THE ROSE

Fragrant clouds seduce my brain with sultry beauty
You are the image of my youthful innocence
Let me sense once more your sweet perfume,
To feel the rush of nature's perfect
A sublime moment of sheer delight.

THE BEE

The humming, humble bee kisses my ears with sweet summer sound
Working with diligence through every nectar flower,
Each anther delicately caressed
As whirring wings orchestrate their resonant chorus
In Mother Nature's theatre of life.
When my karma is complete,
I will return to the great hive of eternity.
(Writing this gave me a buzz.)

THE MOUSE

Who knows the message on sensitive whiskers

The being within the tiny form

Taking its place on Planet Earth,

Seductress of the stealthy cat

Picked off by the ghostly owl

And lured by chocolate into the mortal trap.

Yet we love and deride these creatures

From ancient time into eternity.

PARADISE BIRD

In the jungle depths, the jewels gather and lek, the dance of diamonds and emeralds to

perform. Extroverts, shamans of the avian world, they shimmer, entice and illuminate. It is an act of love fuelled by time, and has outlived the dawn of man. The pure psychedelia of the performance must be a pinnacle of evolution, or a mysterious act of creation, and

unsurpassed as a spectacle of beauty. Little wonder that men believe in other worldly gods.

THE BAT

A bat, the devil's own, flies from behind the sun

Bringing eerie mystery to the night air

Ancient symbol folklores spawn

The moth will die before the dawn

Shall I challenge his satanic mask?

This is all the angels will ask.

Or is he just a flying mouse

An ancient being above the house?

THE FIREFLY

Firefly glow with your incandescent magic

Burn your phosphorescent soul in the night sky

Your life so short, burned with beauty

We in our complexity yearn for simplicity

Yet cannot match the unworldly wonder of your spirit

You are the eternal jewel of the Earth Mother.

THE FOX

A fox is poised with cunning intent

The vole's last energies will soon be spent

Old Reynard coils in deathly dance

This was the creature's very last chance

The circle of life is made complete

Mother Nature's will secrete.

THE WOLF

Wolf cry howling in the night

Under the moon and the stars' cold light

Maligned by man, nature's savage

A lonely deer he will surely ravage

Fiend or devil, his spirit lives on

He flows with the wind, the earth, the sun.

THE SKYLARK

Skylark exulting in the heavens

Lift my spirit up into the sky

Send me on pulsating wings to the far reaches of the cosmos

Unite me with the earth, the sun, the stars

Sing your song of paradise

Let me join infinity, eternity and time

Take me to the sacred place where words cannot reach

Join me on the edge of being

Unite my soul with transcendent beauty.

THE WIND

The wind is my mistress, she stirs my soul

Brings fire to my eyes

Embracing my aching body with warm summer breezes

She is the elemental mother that unites me with fire, water and air

I float along like a silken zephyr

At one, my spirit soars in rhythm with the universal whole

My ego surrenders to the cosmic ebb and flow.

BEAUTY

Take me to the heart of a rainbow

The pulse at the centre of the sun

Ride on the wing of a butterfly

Dance on a water lily

Be burned by the eye of a tiger's eye

Capture it all, feel it, absorb it

With the power of the conscious mind

It is nature's gift in perfect form.

IV

The Eccentric Gardener

DERBYSHIRE

My teens saw me at Spondon Park Grammar, where the cloistered world of enforced academia was an indoor threat and intrusion into the world of a spirit which needed intimate contact with the great outdoors. My best pal Shinny and I would engage in rebellious acts of subversive mischief to offset the formal pressures and disciplines imposed by the establishment. A love of plants grew with the fragrance of each rose I cultivated, the intoxicating fragrance of fragrant cloud, an exquisite rose that lingers as my favourite.

The day of the careers convention dawned, and the apt consequence was a five-year apprenticeship with Derby parks. With intense self-consciousness I started at Darley Abbey, a seat of great learning personified by some wonderful characters, reminders and remnants of the Victorian age, when exotic plants lent sophistication to the landed gentry. I recall the strict and masterful head gardener John Gray, the kindly and expert foreman Ken Hodgkinson and the shrewd, cynical and wise Dennis Morford. All these men held deeply esoteric knowledge of horticulture and were catalysts of compulsive learning.

SKEGNESS

At a very early age my little eyes met the sensation of sweet william blooms. I was absorbed and transfixed, and the image remains some 62 years later. Alert to every facet of nature, Mother pushed the pram towards the council pond, where tiny and magical sticklebacks clung to worms suspended from cotton on sticks. I noticed the cotton wool seed encasings of poplars shimmering in the gentle warm breeze. My feelings for nature went deep and became profound.

We then moved to Skendleby in the Lincolnshire Wolds. Here in the village that time forgot, I meditated in total abstraction on the spring bulbs, with concentration as deep as the time lapse of a young mind, watching each perfect petal open in the garden of delights. An insatiable urge saw me with a spade in the neighbour's wood as I added more snowdrops to our collection. It was clandestine and audacious and very satisfying. In our three acres of orchard, paddocks and gardens I lived out the boy's adventure tale in sweet harmony and at one with the trees, birds, plants and the vibrancy of life. This dreamlike state, occasionally interrupted by adults, would last for five formative years. Part of my soul still haunts that village.

ASKHAM BRYAN

At the introverted and naive age of 18 years I flew the nest and landed at Askham Bryan College for two intense years of solid study and self-indulgence, truly intoxicated by my horticultural enthusiasm in the seat of advanced learning. My time as an aloof and detached bookworm was punctuated by some remarkable incidences. Walking out one day and absorbed in local woods I found a baby crow, and decided that it could live in a box on the window sill of my cloister-room, no. 31 of the new hostels. The cleaning lady was checking out the fluff from under the bed when she shrieked with shock as the bird uttered an almighty caw from the depths of its box. I faced the music over that from the Vice Principal, who asserted that keeping a live crow in my room was taking a love of nature a little too far! That night I went out into the grounds and plucked a young woodpigeon out of a hawthorn tree for good measure.

Sports day between us 'hortics' was an epic encounter against the predominant 'agrics', as we won in pathetic style the slow bicycle race and the cricket-ball throwing contests, where I broke the college record, winning a minute cup in the process. At this time I remained unbeaten at arm wrestling.

Wednesday afternoons were notable for our indulgences in rough shooting on the estate – I kept my 12-bore and bandolier of cartridges in the wardrobe of my room (it was 1968). I loved this primal and focused activity for its elemental and instinctual outlet for a young tyke's inner nature. The dressing of two hares in my room was perhaps a little archaic.

The meals served on wooden benches by adorable and homely cooks were beautiful, and the atmosphere encapsulated by the suckling pig ceremony was institutional, historic and awesome in its spectacle. Our every whim was satisfied: coffee made with milk, a snooker room, juke box and every conceivable delight. I graduated with distinction and secured a place in London at the hallowed and exotic Royal Botanic Gardens, Kew.

KEW, LONDON

The 6th of October 1969 heralded a dramatic three-year period of my life. My beloved roller pigeons, my shooting interests and gentle times in wild countryside would be sacrificed as I morphed kicking and screaming into an institutionalised student. The pursuit of perfection in my subjects resulted in 5 honours in the first year (top student) and there were some gifted people, including a certain Alan Titchmarsh, who shared my digs for a while – a sanguine and affable fellow, driven towards the top.

Although hating the claustrophobia of London, I encountered some great and influential characters. Arthur, a male anorexic, worked in the quaint and lovely rhododendron dell. On a bench I shared his pack as he related experiences of the hippy trail to Marrakesh, India and Kathmandu. Later, my visits to these distant lands would open my eyes to the world of exotica, adventure and danger.

I soon tapped into the rich and diverse humanity on offer at Kew. The Jamaican lads, Little Tom and Big Tom, were outstanding – laid back, laconic and a beautiful alternative to the strident, assertive, compulsive and materialistic Westerners. These boys exemplified the rich colour of a happy-go-lucky personality, and I will always remember them. A character from the South West peninsula intrigued my naive curiosity with his cannabis plants, carefully tied, staked and cultivated in a shrubbery by the Kew wall. I confess to scaling that wall mid-afternoon to meet my young flame, the daughter of a Harley Street doctor, sadly killed in the Trident crash of 1972. We listened to the seminal sounds of Stairway to Heaven composed by genius Jimmy Page. Socialising with Alan Wilton, Bletsoe, Trafford and Tim Spurgeon immersed me in the rock and psychedelic subculture, culminating in mind-altering trips to the 70 Isle of Wight Festival with shaman Hendrix, The Who at Hammersmith Palais for two quid, and memorable musical odysseys by Deep Purple, Stephane Grappelli and the Moody Blues. I was metamorphosing from a sensitive country boy into a rather urbane young man – not before time.

To my chagrin, a little narcolepsy interrupted procedures as I would fall asleep on the seductive hot water pipes that warmed the tropical pits. After three memorable, academically-crazed and hard years I left to go to Worcester College, the first student to do so, for a post-graduation one-year course in rural studies teacher training. Thanks to Leo Pemberton and all the luminous intellects of the great Royal Botanic Gardens Kew.

WORCESTER COLLEGE

My orgy of educational studies continued in teacher training, where I was fortunate enough to mix with some very bright people including an Oxford graduate. I enjoyed the ecological and psychological aspects of the teachers' course and was further obsessed by the whole ethos of being a student, while the gardening aspects were easy. Having friends in the Romany world, and from my life in the countryside, I did a little project on the customs and habits of gypsies, with a romantic notion of their ancient ways. A good friend I shared rooms with was a large man of great wit and charm, and his jovial humour resonated deep within – a lovely man. The pressures were large and I developed some lasting quirks of personality. As usual we were indulged in every corner of our beings.

Suffering from a broken heart in the romantic stakes, I did not excel in the ladies department, and there were some beauties. I recall my digs pal, a nice journalist fellow who worked on the News of the World and loved Eric Clapton. With the company I kept my thinking became more and more intellectual, and my vocabulary expanded with the bright young things that were encountered. Academia took its hold as the morph from practical gardening took effect.

After graduation I took a job at Rugeley and left promptly to work on building sites in Staffordshire and Birmingham, mixing with hard cases, gentlemen and ruffians. The body bristled with muscle, and I had escaped the cloister of formal education. As free as a bird, I became a zoo keeper at Tamworth, living with the ape man in a caravan, and promptly got the sac. It was an education in real life, with a love of characters that has loomed large until today.

SOUTHAMPTON

I returned to my gardening roots in Southampton. My appointment
for Southampton Parks by Terry Ball was bizarre, since I had
initiated him being tossed into the bath fully clothed at Askham
Bryan College. A slick and smart man, he did not harbour a
grudge. My work included The Cedars welfare home, a cosy,
intimate little job where the matron was the mother-in-law of Mick
Channon of racing and football fame. My immediate foreman was
Godfrey, a total gent and a performing magician, being a member
of the Inner Magic Circle. We hit it off, and I toiled and slogged
away at hard labour. I was snoozing away in a shed when they
came to promote me.

In charge I came across Pete the Crook; a scarred face from a knife
attack reflected a history of burglary of posh houses which he was
proud to point out. We hit it off and he would pop into the bulrushes
to smoke a joint at dinner time. A young and driven workaholic, I did
three jobs – pool attendant, fun train driver, and chargehand
gardener. Proud was the day when Pete and I walked into the
showroom and I said 'I'll have that one', a Triumph Spitfire 1500 in
topaz. We swanned around like two wide boys. In the evenings I was
studying social sciences and then humanities at degree level.

When Derby Road was featured in the News of the World, I duly
indulged in a visit to an Australian lady of the red light, an
experience which was shocking and sleazy. But mostly it was work,
work, work and more addictive, obsessive work. I declined any
further promotions and returned to The Cedars for a life of peace
away from the city bustle. My cultural life was enhanced by study
summer schools at Norwich and Stirling universities. My reading
now was Dostoevsky, Kafka, Lawrence and the great artists. From
the seat of science my journey into the arts and humanities paved
the way to my current life as MENSA writer and poet, with a
peculiar specialism in racing pigeons, in which I enjoy a little fame.
In 1976 we returned to York for my fascinating years in the life of an
eccentric gardener

YORK

In the summer of '68 a studious young man toiled in all weathers in the York parks for little pay. I was polite, naive and bright-eyed. Soon I encountered a foreman, a kind and good-natured man called Peter Cook. As a break from the mindless and back-breaking work he took me to his home for tea and a peer at his much-loved cacti and tomato plants. Convinced life was all conscientious hard grind, I recall the man now with affection. Oh that all middle management would prove to be his equal!

On and off I put in the years with sweat blood and tears until a pivotal and life changing day in February of '96. Working at the expansive, open space of Rowntree Park there were some colourful and memorable events. I attempted to tow Bob, the man in charge, using my Minivan to bump start the antiquated Bonza truck. This was a dramatic success, as it ripped part of the back of the van off. Bob to his credit was an honest man, although touched by some nervous quirks.

We formed a cunning plan to cull the resident garden fantail flock down to the bright and healthy specimens. This murderous spree was rumbled by the resident park keeper and it created a furore extending to the Chief Executive of the council. To this day I respect the fact that poor old Bob took it on the chin.

A jovial character called Charlie worked in the park. In an ambitious attempt to light a stove, traces of fuel found their way on to his hair and caught fire – I extinguished it with raw speed.

Young and wild, I had returned from a spirited and free trip to the Himalayas, departing overland from London. I was like the Wild Man of Borneo with long hair and outlandish clothes to match. Dennis, a complex and outrageous character, under the influence of red mist, drove the garden truck through the basement doors, narrowly missing my feet. This caused some consternation in camp. The irony was that I talked my way to promotion at West Park, where the events kicked off.

As I was an aspiring union man, the hierarchy loathed my impact on the organisation. In time I reached the dizzy heights of convenor of all the unions in York City Council employ. I worked on principle and from the social perspective of the rights, needs and desires of the working staff. I relished the role and led the dynamic and successful manual worker review of 1988. This entailed meticulous planning and negotiations at the highest level to achieve.

In the final analysis, after many years of repeated toil to do my best, I surrendered to stress, and the personnel section, in their compassion and wisdom, allowed me to retire. My thanks go out to everyone who helped me on the path to freedom.

V

Legends

LEGEND I

With fists of fury and a giant ego, this Narcissus became the most famous man on planet earth. His psychopathic intensity of resolve, his poetic wit and charm enthralled a generation of converts to his mesmerising personality. With deep-seated, moral convictions he rocked the American establishment. Now in age and frailty, he still transcends the sport in which he ruled so elegantly. I give you a man of singular individuation: Muhammad Ali.

LEGEND II

A person of acute hypersensitivity captured an image, the quintessence of trauma, angst and sensory overload. Created back in historical time, it looms large in the sensibility of 21st century schizoid man. Millions of people at the mercy of Western capitalism, subservient to the money god, feel its raw, intuitive power. It remains an enduring symbol of profound, deep, psychic disturbance, the epitome of emotional distress, at the heart of jostling humanity. Bordering on abject psychosis, I refer to The Scream by Edvard Munch.

LEGEND III

With sublime feet of mercurial artistry, his abiding presence on the field of dreams was the grace and flow of pure beauty. With a refined, masculine charm, he seduced the rich and the beautiful and held Miss Worlds in the palm of his hand, all enchanted by his handsome charisma. But behind the mask of genius lurked a demon, satisfied only by the ingestion of ethyl alcohol. Although he died racked and ravaged by self-indulgent excess, his place in football folklore is secure, and the intensity of his star will never fade. Simply the best – I whisper the name of George Best.

LEGEND IV

Florid outpourings from the inner cavern of restless madness daubed the canvas in brilliant hues of gold and green. The feverish spirit of the inner man, a cauldron of shadowy demons, sought solace and pure calm in externalisation on canvas to satiate and quell the inner torment. Visual images were not sufficient, so this desperate soul terminated his earthly suffering, leaving an enduring legacy of dynamic form and colour, exemplified by the famous Sunflowers. We now immortalise the expressive power, the inner vision of an intuitive giant, the great Vincent Van Gogh.

LEGEND V

Her flame has burned in the memory of popular culture ever since she beguiled a generation with her hair of gold. She became a living archetype of desire as her female form ignited the lust and admiration of a generation. Pawn of the political and power-crazed elite, she shimmered on the silver screen. Now she shines in our galaxy of memories, her earthly life snuffed out under a cloak of suspicion and secrecy. She endures, protected by a rich vein of history, known only as Marilyn Monroe.

LEGEND VI

This man, fuelled by a profound, psychotic fervour, galvanised the needy and vulnerable masses of a nation. With the fires of persuasive oratory, he acted out his deluded and destructive fantasies on ethnic groups in a faraway dream to purify and perfect the Aryan race. This insane dogma spawned a mass campaign of institutionalised genocide. His name remains the axis of megalomaniac evil, and his physical demise remains shrouded in mystery. He remains the benchmark by which other despots are judged. I refer to Adolf Hitler.

LEGEND VII

Next and final legend: A man of sublime egocentricity and musical acumen, he presides over the entertainment as a colossus. Sure and ruthless, he inspires rejection and devotion, and total attention to purpose. A musical generation of stars is born from the seat of his consciousness, to shine in the mainstream of pop culture. He is a personification of the will to power and the triumph of the individual over the dross of mediocracy. This awesome human is Simon Cowell.

VI

Days that changed my life

In Chicken Street in Kabul, transfixed by a seedy and shady rogue, I was drawn by intense fascination into the den of narcotic vice. Unable to control an inner yearning, and with adventurous curiosity, I bought a solid lump of the black tar of euphoria-street opium. Retiring to my hotel bed, I waited for the life-threatening, deep sleep of dreams, induced by that wicked witch of a poppy flower, whose power is masked behind delicate blooms.

Anxious American traveller friends searched for the fading pulse and heartbeat; was the flower to claim another victim? Then the renaissance. I awoke light, euphoric, ethereal and empowered from within, to begin my incredible journey back to life, from the nothing I had become.

◊ ◊ ◊ ◊ ◊

Early morning, soulful, detached and serene, I emerged from the dark night and stepped out into ornate, scented gardens for the blind. The cool, crystal air tingled my nostrils with an exhilarating freshness. In one beautiful and timeless moment, I raised my head towards the sky. Penetrating, piercing and pondering the white cotton wool clouds, kissed by the rising sun, first the rush of sweet euphoria, then the awesome realisation that my miniscule, insignificant self was looked down upon by the snow-clad peaks of ANNAPURNA. The impact was a revelation, a spiritual communion with the cosmos.

◊ ◊ ◊ ◊ ◊

I loved to go where the curlew cries and the wild geese fly over sunset skies. Way back in the wilderness, alive, alone, hidden by a tidal creek, my senses were alerted by an approaching chorus of pink-footed geese. With the sea lavender kissed by the September sun, the birds, fresh from summer pasture in Greenland, were eerily early. My call to them echoed across the silent expanse of the Wash saltings. In joyous anticipation I sensed the skein approaching, me.

The singular wildfowler, poised in motionless anticipation of their arrival. A single flash from the trusty twelve hit the rapidly-disappearing target. Man and nature were united by this ancient ritual, the wild goose chase. A record early goose, it launched my writing career and taught me well about respect, life and death in the presence of solitude.

Waiting in silent anticipation, would my bird battle against the vagaries of wind, rain and tide to return from the epic endurance race of the Barcelona International? On the edge of possibility, was I about to cover myself in glory, the realisation of a dream with my little feathered champion? In the dark and stirring restlessness of the night time, the brain was charged by bolts of electricity, like the lightning of possibilities. The day saw a swirling pool of unfulfilled emotions that defied control. And then, in the setting sun, the swooping down of the old cock bird, the rush of heady euphoria and the gradual realisation that this great feat would change my life forever. Those days are the nectar of my nostalgia

On a lake that shimmered and twinkled in bliss, my eye was filled with the majesty of a lone eagle that soared with effortless grace above the snowy peaks of Kashmir. From beneath the pristine, calm waters silver fish boiled in a frenzy of feeding on wriggling life forms, cloaked in deep green algae. In serene contemplation, I found my significance, as part of the whole, an enduring and inner spiritual metamorphosis. A flood of florid brilliance suffused my senses as exotic kingfishers mesmerised me, diving into the lake of plenty. My calling would be an aesthete who aimed to recapture such sublime moments and treasures of the earth.

Waiting in silent anticipation, would my bird battle against the vagaries of wind,

rain and tide to return from the epic endurance race of the Barcelona International?

On the edge of possibility, was I about to cover myself in glory, the realisation of a dream with my little feathered champion?

In the dark and stirring restlessness of the night time, the brain was charged by bolts of electricity, like the lightning of possibilities.

The day saw a swirling pool of unfulfilled emotions that defied control. And then, in the setting sun, the swooping down of the old cock bird, the rush of heady euphoria and the gradual realisation that this great feat would change my life forever.

Those days are the nectar of my nostalgia.

Dark and painful memories may fade a little, with the mists of time, yet one is cemented deep in the archives, the well of the brain.

In 72, in the absorbing company of an old flame, I sat in vague indifference to the TV medium until a far-reaching and penetrating news flash - a plane had fallen from the skies.

The emergent shock seized my friend, as the crippled hand of fate chose her for the heavy blow of painful reality. The physical reminders of her doctor father were his bible and pen.

Blessed are those who can match emotional pain with spiritual resistance. The highest good is like water; it dwells in places that many men despise.

Printed in Great Britain
by Amazon

62956739R00068